The Practical (And Indispensable!) Pastor's Handbook:

Exploring What You Actually Need To Do As A 21st-Century Minister

Brian A. Ross

CSS Publishing Company, Inc.
Lima, OH

The Practical (And Indispensable!) Pastor's Handbook:

Library of Congress Cataloging-in-Publication Data:
Names: Ross, Brian A., author. Title: The practical (and indispensable!) pastor's handbook: : exploring what you actually need to do as a 21st-century minister / Brian A. Ross. Other titles: Practical pastor's handbook Description: Lima, OH : CSS Publishing Company, Inc., 2020. | Summary: "The Practical (and Indispensable!) Pastor's Handbook: Exploring What You Actually Need to Do as a 21st Century Minister offers an extremely practical "how to" guide for the most common activities of younger, contemporary pastors. As a nineteen-year ministry veteran, all of the material here was honed through my initially difficult (and yet ultimately successful) experience as a church planter in a region that was not initially friendly to church ministry"-- Provided by publisher. Identifiers: LCCN 2020000269 | ISBN 9780788029523 (paperback) | ISBN 9780788029547 (ebook) Subjects: LCSH: Pastoral theology--Handbooks, manuals, etc. Classification: LCC BV4011.3 .R676 2020 | DDC 253--dc23 LC record available at https://lccn.loc.gov/2020000269

For more information about CSS Publishing Company resources, visit our website at www.csspub.com or email us at csr@csspub.com or call (800) 241-4056.

eBook:
ISBN-13: 978-07880-2954-7
ISBN-10: 0-7880-2954-1

ISBN-13: 978-0-78803-101-4

DIGITALLY PRINTED

Contents

Handling Pastoral And Self-Care

Introduction (A Confession)

I don't read books like this one. I don't like books like this one. I advise my students to largely avoid books like this one. This book, that I have written, somewhat troubles *me*.

This book is way too pragmatic, programmatic, and even somewhat shallow. Church ministry is infinitely more complicated than this book presupposes and the valid approaches to church ministry are immensely more varied than this one.

Then there is the *title*....

When I first made the massive transition from serving as a lead pastor to a full-time seminary professor, moving nearly 3,000 miles, I reached out to local church leaders in my new community —Fresno, California. I made these connections partly to hear from those who were ministering on the ground, and partly, to connect with others with whom I had much in common. Repeatedly these ministry leaders made the same request: "Could you please teach your students to do, what pastors, actually do? Seminary graduates certainly know their bible and theology, but they often do not know how to do anything in the church!"

After hearing these sentiments, and after conferring with my colleague Dr. Lynn Jost, I set out to put in print "everything" that a new senior or solo pastor needs to know how to do. After a few weeks, and a few versions of different lists, the outline for what became this manual emerged. When I finished, and I looked over all of the pastoral pragmatics, I felt somewhat embarrassed at what I had sketched out.

The self-interrogation began: *What is a metaphysical day-dreamer, like yourself, doing creating a "how to" manual? Isn't this too simple, too basic? Isn't it bordering on idolatry to insist that you have captured and bottled up the manifold experience of human beings within the church? Should this not include theological reflections? Prayerful spirituality? You know, Brian, your students are going to roll their eyes at you and drop your courses after their first class....*

Despite my misgivings, I went with it. To my surprise, most of my students appreciated the work. I began to hear several, "Oh, now that makes sense..." and "I never thought of that before..." I heard, "You can do ministry like this?" and, "Okay, now I feel like I am getting a handle on what the craft of ministry looks like…" Veteran pastors (who have been slowly working on their seminary degree for quite some time) remarked: "I have been in ministry for years and yet I am gaining some fresh insights as to what we could do differently and more effectively." My most intellectually gifted student simply asked: "Brian, why have you not published this material?"

I have been surprised at how this work has seem to benefit many. My only guess is that as Baby Boomer church leaders obsessed over the pragmatics of developing large and successful ministries, we Gen Xers felt grossed out and went in the other direction. Now, a generation later, younger church leaders despite their earnestness, inclusive approaches, and more nuanced theological sophistication, have lost some of the simple "how to do ministry" principles and practices.

Maybe I should revise my statement above? This book, that I have written, somewhat embarrasses me- *but not enough to keep me from publishing it.*

I am confident that any reader of this manual, will disagree with its contents at various junctures.

"My church doesn't do what you're saying… and it still works for us!"

"The author's particular theological tradition is nakedly exposed here…"

"This section, would never work in my context."

"Why does the author assume that HIS way is THE way?"

Any of these types of accusations and reactions are to be expected. Of course, there is not one "right way" to minister. Of course, there are things that I am missing. Of course, some have likely taken the opposite approach of what I have suggested here and the Spirit has still moved on a grand scale. Of course.

You will be right — I do come across in this text like I know exactly what you should do. But I don't. This manual is written as if I was asked to give advice to someone who is taking on these tasks *as if for the first time.* A simple: *do this and don't do that,* seemed like the easiest approach to take. How many times could I say: *Well, maybe, possibly, in the right situation, you might consider… but you do not have to…*

Despite my admission of how this manual makes me a bit uneasy, I still believe that it belongs on the shelf of younger pastors, seminary, and Bible college students, and even church board members and key lay leaders. Our age is long on theory and short on thought-through approaches for the honing of craft. Long on good intentions and short on follow through. Long on ideals and short on walking them into action.

This manual has been cobbled together from a mash-up of my experience as a church planter and lead pastor, my study as a working minister and seminary professor, and my observations in checking in on ministries all over North America and in worshiping in dozens and dozens of different congregations over the last few years. Much of the counsel that it offers I have personally practiced. Where I have not personally implemented its suggestions — I wish that I had.

This book is far from complete or perfect. But that does not mean that it be should neglected. *Indispensable?* Doubtful. *A helpful guide?* Probably.

Handling Sundays

Designing Worship Gatherings

A step-by-step guide to the brainstorming and planning of public worship services that includes suggested order(s) of service, how far out planning must begin, and more.

"Worship... needs to be characterized by hospitality; it needs to be inviting. But at the same time, it should be inviting seekers into the church and its unique story and language. Worship should be an occasion of cross-cultural hospitality."

-James K. A. Smith

"Worship evangelism is Christians worshiping the one true God in front of nonbelievers."

-Sally Morganthaler

"Everything should be done in a fitting and orderly way."

-1 Corinthians 14:40

Importance:
-Most people who either visit your church, or who are regularly involved with the church, make Sunday public worship their main priority. Almost always, it serves as *home base* for regulars and as the *front door* for new people.

-Therefore, get very *hands on* with designing worship experiences. See yourself as the main "producer" of the gathering. Be sure that people find "enough of what they are looking for" (hope, wisdom, and friends) and what you would like them to find: *God*. There are many aspects of ministry (most aspects of ministry) that should be entrusted to other people by the pastor. This is *not* one of them.

Practices That Are (Almost) Always True:
-Every worship gathering must include: musical worship/singing, a sermon, and some form of prayer.

-Begin worship with some form of *up-beat* or *energizing* song set. Most people need to be woken up and energized. They do come to church for something *positive* and hopeful. As a rule, whomever is leading worship sets the tone at the beginning. (They need to bring energy and enthusiasm if they want others to experience it.)

-Conversely, the final song (before the sermon) should *bring things down* a bit to prepare people to hear from the word of God. Musical worship is *more* than simply moving people's emotions — but it is certainly not *less* than that.

-You will want to offer *some* variety from Sunday to Sunday (or people will get bored rather quickly). However, human beings are creatures of habit. They are expecting *some* consistency in worship from Sunday to Sunday. (For example, some people will always show up late, intentionally, to miss musical worship.) If you change it up too much, you will frustrate people.

-Additionally, most potential visitors want to have a general idea of what will happen before they decide to venture out and check out your church. It helps to have a general description on the church website.

A Possible Order of Worship (Contemporary):

>3 Songs
>Announcements/Offering
>Song
>Pop-Culture Element
>Sermon
>Q And A
>Prayer/Communion, and the like

A Possible Order of Worship (Liturgical):

>Song
>Welcome
>Song
>Call to Confession/Assurance of Pardon
>Song
>Passing of the Peace
>Scripture Reading
>Sermon
>Song
>Offering/Music
>Prayer/Communion

Song
Benediction

Practices That Are (Likely) True, Or At Least Helpful (Most Of The Time):

-Announcements can easily "ruin the mood" of public worship. Because of this, some churches opt to begin worship with them or end with them. The potential problem with these time slots is that many people will not hear what is being shared. They are either arriving late, or are already on the way out. One way of dealing with this is to imbed announcements in the middle of a worship song set. The only slight problem with this is that the worship team often feel that it disrupts their process.

-Be sure to "preach" the announcements. A hack gets up there and just shares what is going on and/or reads the bulletin. A seasoned veteran plans ahead of time, and thinks through what they are going to say and why and how. They work to make announcements interesting and effective. It *does* matter that people know what is going on with the church. But you cannot highlight everything. Announcing *everything* is the same thing as announcing *nothing*.

-DO pass offering plates. Churches tend to receive around 15-20% more of an offering if they pass plates during worship instead of simply offering "boxes" in the corner. Many people will spontaneously give if plates are passed. (They should also be able to give privately, give through direct deposit, give through texting apps, also.)

Planning Ahead:

-Plan sermons six months out to give the worship team time to prepare.

-Consider utilizing a "creative" team. Invite a handful of people with a background in the arts, pop culture, etc. to meet with you every couple of months to brainstorm elements for worship. This can be quite helpful. Sadly, creative people are often underutilized in churches.

-The latest that a Sunday schedule should be sent out to everyone involved is Tuesday. (Large churches plan these out much earlier.) You cannot do anything well if it is rushed and finalized at the last minute. Special services like Christmas Eve or Easter should be planned months in advance.

-Worship plans need to be scheduled out to the smallest level of detail. How long worship lasts will depend on your tradition, but for experiences to be meaningful, they often should be thoroughly scheduled and planned out. Some churches plan down to the minute!

-Provide detailed instructions for all of those who are involved in leading worship. Yes, it can be a pain, but if you don't, people will be confused and will struggle to facilitate worship that is meaningful. Never *assume* that people know what to do or know what you are looking for. Along with the schedule, it can be helpful to send a paragraph or two, with detailed instructions, for those who are leading various aspects of the gathering.

-I suggest that you outline worship personally — as the senior pastor but some others do it as a team.

Other Elements:

-Think through your philosophy of worship leading, corporate prayer, announcements, and more. You need to communicate to others who facilitate worship the *why* of what they are doing. It is not simply *what* is said or sung. But also, *how* it is said or sung, and to *whom*, all according to *what* you are trying to accomplish.

-If "normal" people share their story, or if you dedicate a child, or if you are a celebrating something amazing that the church took on within the neighborhood — these are often best experienced *before* the sermon.

-Baptisms, financial updates, communion, interactive prayers, and more are often most helpful *after* the sermon. (And you *always* want to have something meaningful, spiritual, and participatory after the sermon.)

Participatory Worship Instead Of A Worship Performance

Contemporary people do not to sit and watch, they long to engage. Suggestions are offered to make public worship more experiential and less passive.

"It is easy to fail when designing an interactive experience. Designers fail when they do not know the audience, integrate the threads of content and context, welcome the public properly, or make clear what the experience is and what the audience's role in it will be."

-Edwin Schlossberg

"I tell my son, who's a producer, 'You never work for the machine; the machine works for you.'"

-Quincy Jones

"Let the message of Christ dwell among you richly as you teach and admonish one another with all wisdom through psalms, hymns, and songs from the Spirit, singing to God with gratitude in your hearts."

-Colossians 3:16

Reason and Purpose:
One of the major shifts within our times is that most people are are now accustomed to the posture of "participation". Smart phones are now a consistent part of life. These are quite literally changing the ways that our brains are hard-wired. We are no longer a people who are content to *watch* and *observe*. We desire to *interact* and *participate*. To ignore this changing human reality, can lead us to design and facilitate worship services that are increasingly experienced as meaningless, ineffectual, and a complete waste of time.

-To facilitate "participatory" worship is to adopt a philosophy of ministry that seeks to create a *context* where the Spirit just might move in the lives of people. It is largely not "telling" or "instructing" or "performing" for people. It is creating a context, where the unpredictable Spirit may work within people. This *does* involve a level of giving up control, or at least, letting go of the concept that it is our job to control what people *get* from worship. (As if we could have ever controlled this!) Experienced ministers know that what God does in people's lives is rarely what we expected that God would do. Why? (Besides, He is God and we are not.) Every person comes to worship with a different backstory, different struggles in the moment, different personalities — therefore, we cannot plan or predict what God *should* do within their lives during worship.

Forms Of Participatory Worship That Often Seem To "Pop":

-Taking communion/Eucharist — particularly "up front." (People getting out of their seats to receive the bread and cup, complete with a blessing from those who are serving.)

-Laying hands on people in prayer. (This tactile posture of inscribing worth, and calling on the Spirit to move powerfully, can be deeply meaningful.)

-Leading people in a personal time of prayer. (Music playing softly, and guiding people in how to pray and connect with God right where they are.)

-Q And A with the preacher after the sermon. (Parishioners can ask questions, make comments, etc. through an open-mic period after the sermon. People often really enjoy this even if they do not personally participate. It is certainly interesting — but it also communicates that the church is an open place and not afraid of different perspectives and experiences.)

-"Normal" people sharing their personal stories publicly. (This can be deeply moving — they do not need people. And they do *not* have to all be Christians to share.)

Other Forms Of Participatory Worship (That May Or May Not Work):

-Responsive readings. (Certainly participatory — but can be a bit boring. These can be too "word-centered" instead of image-based or participatory.)

-Using the body in prayer. (Kneeling, and other movements can work in some churches, while not in others.)

-People discussing a question in small groups at their seats. (This can work well — if it is not experienced too often.)

-Creative group art projects. (Innovative? Yes. But hard to do well and to keep from being too cheesy.)

-Various "get up and do" tasks. (Get up and give someone a hug. Get up and light a candle. These can work and can also be weird.)

Methods Of Preaching That Feel Participatory:
-Object lessons

-Using images that correspond with the teaching

-Asking open-ended questions

-Telling stories (psychologically people begin to think about their own lives when they hear about someone else's)

-Describing the listeners' lives, and how they think, back to them (as if from the inside)

-Giving voice to questions that you know people have

-Ample use of metaphors

Other Thoughts:
-Increasingly, some people are beginning to prepare their sermons, with others, as a team. This way, multiple perspectives go into the crafting of a sermon which makes it more likely that you will connect with different kinds of people. However, this also has the potential to water down sermons by lessening the power of preaching through a particular personality.

-To create a context where the Spirit can work — you should be thoroughly prepared. Think through all the details and explanations and directions — to not confuse others. Meaningful spontaneous experiences are often, highly planned.

-It's invaluable to develop a team of people who can help you to brainstorm and create different participatory practices. Use the gifts that are there in your church.

Making Announcements
(And Yes) Taking An Offering

The author maintains that nothing should be "winged" during Sunday worship. Even the ins and outs of announcements and the collection of tithes and offerings should be well thought through ahead of time.

"People do not buy goods and services. They buy relations, stories and magic."

-Seth Godin

"The first problem of communication is getting people's attention."

-Chip And Dan Heath

"Now about the collection for the Lord's people: Do what I told the Galatian churches to do. On the first day of every week, each one of you should set aside a sum of money in keeping with your income."

-1 Corinthians 16:1-2

Announcements:
-Sometimes, the only difference between meaningful Sunday worship and an experience that is rather forgettable is how much attention is paid to the small details. Giving real attention to thinking through Sunday morning announcements, being sure that communication is clear, interesting, and relevant, may not seem terribly important — but it is. Whatever you do, do not simply wing announcements. Do not waste any opportunity when you have people's attention during a public Sunday gathering. Every aspect communicates more than you know to those who are gathered. *Are these people interesting? Do these people care enough about what they are doing — to do it with excellence? Do these people understand me? Is church worth showing up for or is it as boring and as irrelevant as I feared?* How people think about the *church* — often determines how they think about *Jesus*.

Content Of Announcements:

-Give an appropriate amount of the *why* the church is engaged in its specific activities. (But do not go *too long* — this has a reverse effect.) Make sure that whomever shares during announcements is someone who has the ability to speak in front of others —otherwise, people will not hear what they are trying to say. (Poor public communication is terribly distracting.) Occasionally, it may be helpful if the senior pastor offers announcements — it provides extra heft to a special event when that is needed. However, in general, announcements offer a great opportunity for *someone else* to share. You do not want Sunday morning to become "the pastor show."

-Some churches offer an "open announcement time" where anyone can share about an upcoming event. The advantage of this is that everyone feels *included* within the church community. The downside is that church leaders may be *diluting* the vision of the church: people are hearing about several different opportunities, which leads people to wonder *what are the priorities around here?* It can also come across as unprofessional. As if you were not thoroughly prepared for the worship experience. This is especially the case for visitors who do not personally know the people who are sharing. Again, when people think you are *unprofessional* they think you are not taking the work/ministry seriously. Which also means that *Jesus* is not worth taking very seriously.

-Be sure to address and give attention to welcome packets during announcements. Explain everything, each week, as if everyone was there for the *first* time.

-Don't read the bulletin, only highlight a couple of key events, which you strategically planned out ahead of time.

-You likely *do* want to hand out a bulletin. People often want to read *something*. Especially *visitors* — they like to have something to do, besides playing the extrovert, when in a new space. If they are not reading your bulletin — they are looking at their smartphone! Besides, people need *multiple* reminders today, to hear anything: public announcements, announcements in print (bulletin), social media, church emails, calendars sent via snail mail, and more.

Announcement Strategy:

-Think through and have a strategic policy regarding what gets into the bulletin, and what is announced on Sundays, and *when*. If you neglect this step, all sorts of people will want all sorts of things printed in the bulletin and announced on Sundays. It's often awkward and difficult to say no to them if there is not already a policy in place.

-There are always trade-offs about *when* to share announcements: at the beginning of worship — many people may not yet have arrived. At the end of worship — some are already running for the doors. In the middle of worship, it can impair the building momentum of the gathering.

Offering:

-All pastors make mistakes. However, you cannot keep your job if you engage in sexual sin, if you mishandle money, and if you *cannot raise* enough money.

-Do not apologize for taking an offering and do pass the plates. Congregants are going to spend their money *somewhere*. If they do not invest in the church, they'll simply go on another vacation or out for drinks a few more times. To downplay financial giving is to simply assure that parishioners give their money to some *corporation* somewhere (buying more things). Besides, if you *believe* in the ministry, you will want it to have a future. How will ministry move forward without enough money coming in to the church?

-Regularly make a point of telling stories of where some of the money is going and *why*. You cannot do this every week, but you can do it regularly. (The more inspiring — the better.)

-Provide clear and *multiple* pathways for people to give financially to the ministry: passing the plate, online, a box in the back, direct deposit, texting apps, and others.

-Keep a highly detailed church budget in the foyer and mail one annually to every member and regular attendee of the church. It is much easier for people to give financially when there are *zero questions* about where money is going. Confusing budgets lead people to distrust the church leaders, which means, they invest much less financially in the ministry.

-Publish giving numbers clearly in the bulletin along with the budget's status *year to date*. (People with jobs and money care about this sort of thing. If you do not do this, serious donors will not take you and the church very seriously.)

| Weekly Budget | $2, 312.00 |
| Weekly Giving (9-9-20) | $1, 980.00 |

| Annual Budget YTD | $83, 232.00 |
| Annual Giving YTD | $82, 836.00 |

Taking The Offering:

-If you pass the plates after the sermon, people are more likely to give, but some people may leave early. If you take the offering earlier, everyone is present, but they may be not quite as motivated to give. I prefer to take the offering during announcements (and after musical worship) while people are hearing all that is happening within the life of the church. But, of course, there is no one right way to do this.

-Be sure that there are giving envelopes at all the seats. Additionally, provide clear and simple info for giving through direct deposit, using texting applications, and more.

Praying Before God
And Before Your Community

All church leaders offer public prayers, few make them meaningful and potentially impactful. The nuts and bolts of pastoral prayers are explored.

"We assume prayer is something to master the way we master algebra or auto mechanics. That puts us in the 'on-top' position, where we are competent and in control. But when praying, we come 'underneath,' where we calmly and deliberately surrender control and become incompetent."

-Richard J. Foster

"We are formed together as we learn to pray together."

-Scot McKnight

"When Paul had finished speaking, he knelt down with all of them and prayed."

-Acts 20:36

Potential And Possible Problems:
-The benefits of leading people in prayer are likely evident:
    1. It is a *participatory* experience that engages people rather than leaving them as mere observers and listeners.
    2. Hopefully people experience a personal encounter with the Spirit.
    3. It is a subtle way of teaching people how to pray and engage God.
-Some of the often overlooked "problems" with public prayer:
    1. The pastor can pray *too long* and it becomes rather boring listening to them pray (and not praying ourselves). This is especially the case when pastoral prayers use words that one "should use," — which do not come across as very authentic.

2. Too many individuals mindlessly pray up front: someone says a prayer in the opening welcome, then the worship leader prays when they walk onto the platform and when they exit, then the pastor prays before and after the sermon, then someone prays for the offering, etc. Many times, leaders offer these prayers not purposefully or intentionally, but because they feel that either they "should" pray or that it works as an acceptable transition mechanism. This can cheapening prayer and give the impression that it is rather meaningless.

3. Assume everyone in public worship knows how to pray and regularly prays. A lack of sensitivity to the unfamiliarity that many normal people have with public spiritual acts can gut public prayer from its effectiveness.

A Few Possible Forms And Methods For Public Prayer:

Leading People In Private Prayer

As a possible response to the sermon, ask people to stand and close their eyes, and to do their best to experiment with talking with God privately. Explain that you are not asking them to say anything *out loud* but to inwardly be honest with God. Guide them in what to pray for. Something like: *"Name to God whatever is causing you pain right now, being as honest with God as you possibly can..."* Give a little direction and then 30 seconds of silence. Then repeat this rhythm a few times. Close the time in prayer yourself. (Music should be softly playing during this time.)

Praying For People Through The Laying On Of Hands

Ask, with everyone's eyes closed (toward the end of a pastoral prayer) if someone is truly hurting to raise their hand. Let them know they do not need to say or do anything, simply raise their hand. Then ask everyone to get up, move toward these people, and lay a hand on them. Ask those who feel comfortable to pray for the person out loud. Acknowledge that this may seem a little strange — but encourage people to give it a try.

Invite People To Come Up Front To Be Prayed For

Invite key church leaders (who have been well trained in advance) to come and stand up front. Invite anyone, who would like prayer for anything (no matter how big or small) to come up front and someone standing there will pray for them. The pray-ers should listen briefly to the issue, avoid offering counsel, but lay a hand on the person and pray for them. This often works best if the congregation is worshipping through music at the same time as these prayer opportunities. (This could also be facilitated in the back of the worship space as well.)

Lead People In A Moment Of Silence

Occasionally it is helpful to remind people of the importance of simply standing before God in silence — acknowledging God's presence, and that we are not God, we live in dependence. Explain the value (confessing that it is a little strange) and simply facilitate people standing, with eyes closed, in silence for a moment while music plays quietly.

Meditative Prayer

Sometimes (if not entered into too regularly) we can teach people how to pray through specific spiritual formation exercises. For example, lead everyone through a brief experience of *lectio divina*, or something similar. This *can* be deeply impactful, *if* it is only experienced occasionally and if the whole experience and its purpose are clearly explained.

Responsive (or "read") Prayers

Choose a deeply authentic prayer from the Christian past. With instruction, reminding people that this is a way to respond to God. Read a line, and then have the congregation read a line and so on. (Their parts will need to be in bold-faced print.) Or, the pastor and congregation could read the entire prayer in unison.

Final Thoughts And Suggestions:

-It is usually best to explain *why* we are praying (how it forms us) and that prayer is not simply a religious rabbit's foot.

-Always *explain* how the church will be praying together (keeping visitors in mind) to help people feel a little more comfortable and able to fully engage.

-Have music playing softly in the background during prayer — it helps to create atmosphere. Music has always been an intricate aspect of spirituality. Music *is* creating a sense of meaning that is beyond words.

-Some churches regularly announce prayer requests from up front. This has the advantage of creating a sense of community. However, it can also be off-putting to guests (especially if you are consistently praying for elderly people's physical ailments.) It may be better to either include these in the bulletin or email prayer chain that people sign up for. Special prayer requests (shared up front) are best reserved for instances of sudden death or grave illness of *younger* people.

Preparing A Sermon That Is Worth Listening To

A "cheat sheet" on preparing sermons that resonate with contemporary people. Rhetorical strategies and delivery methods are covered.

"Stories are the only containers big enough to carry truth, because stories convey not just the facts but also the feelings and the nuances of truth."

-Rick Richardson

"I have come closer to being bored out of the Christian faith than being reasoned out of it. I think we underestimate the deadly gas of boredom. It is not only the death of communication, but the death of life and hope."

-Haddon Robinson

"Seated in a window was a young man named Eutychus, who was sinking into a deep sleep as Paul talked on and on."

-Acts 20:9

Brief Overview Of Constructing A Sermon:
-Without looking at any other resources (commentaries, theological works, or the like) simply pray and read over the chosen passage... slowly. Notice what *pricks* or moves you — not an idea, but a personal revelation. Something that *surprises* you and *challenges* you.

-Prayerfully discern *one* central theme based on the encounter above. Spoken, public, communication can only have *one* main point if it is to be clear to the listeners.

-Ask yourself: *How does this one point grab me personally? What angle could I take with this one point that might "work" with these listeners?* ("Work" means that is draws them in and challenges them at the same time.)

-Prayerfully begin brainstorming over which path the sermon will need to take for you to effectively communicate this one main thing.

Common Forms That Sermons May Take:

-A 3-subpoint sermon, all based on the one main point. The sub-points clearly come from the text. The form is basically: Point, Story/Application, Point, Story/Application, Point, Story/Application.

-A sermon based around one narrative or metaphor. The story or image is shared and then a point or application is made. Then another aspect of the story or image is shared, and then another point or application is made.

-If the sermon is purely topical (not based on a single passage) you will have your work cut out for you! Most topical sermons still cover the 3-subpoint sermon model; however, they reference different passages with each subpoint. (However, multiple texts in one sermon tend to confuse rather than illuminate.)

Generating Material:

-Once you have the main point, and the form you will build around, you need to start putting some flesh on the bones. It is helpful to ask yourself: *What elements do I need to pull this off?* Perhaps you could open with a story that will lead to the topic, provide examples of how people tend to live out these themes or work against it, and mention skeptics' questions, ect.

-As anything comes to mind, write it down. You can edit it and sort it later. (The human brain cannot create and critically edit at the same time.)

-After a long period of prayerful brainstorming (which must be a separate process than editing) begin to look over your outline and cut and add and rearrange.

-Once you are content with the overall outline, illustrations, etc. it is time to write the sermon. This can be literally writing it down or verbalizing it out loud. Regardless, go over it a few times, cutting and editing. (If you write the sermon out, do *not* take the manuscript into the pulpit with you! Eye contact and passion may count more than reading the "just right" word. It is better to read over the manuscript multiple times but only to take a scaled down outline with you into the pulpit.)

Helpful Elements To Consider:

1. Always prepare communication as if plenty of unbelievers are present. Even if they are not, eventually they will show up! This means we cannot use "church-speak" or theological language.

27

Or at least, you will have to work hard to explain it in a way that resonates with listeners.

2. Communicate Jesus and his gospel as a "completely unusual and unique path." Some will assume that when you talk about "what the Bible says" that you are trying to talk them into being conservative and traditional. Others will assume when you talk about love and forgiveness that you are trying to talk them into being liberal and progressive. The only way you can make Jesus clear is to contrast him with both "conservativism" and "progressivism." This will communicate to new people that you are speaking of God — someone who is beyond the agendas of this world. Additionally, this will challenge long-term church people! Jesus-shaped ministry *always* intrigues some outsiders while offending some moralistic people.

3. Well-crafted stories and narratives can touch the heart of skeptics in a way that simple propositions cannot. They invite the listener to imagine the scenario instead of simply analyzing it. The human mind will naturally turn to how they have experienced a similar situation. Truth is communicated skillfully, while giving room for the listener to adjust it to their experience and allowing it to be more personally relevant.

4. People are more likely to "trust you" and consider your message if you can admit where detractors have a point. Admitting and confessing (to an appropriate degree) where some religious people are missing it will help listeners believe that you are authentically trying to communicate truth. Appropriately sharing where you have failed, and how you have been changed by the Spirit, communicates trustworthiness.

5. Use "pop-culture" references and examples when possible. Popular Culture is the "Lingua Franca" of North Americans. This says to listeners that you understand them, you inhabit the same world that they do, that you are not a "weirdo" who simply rails against their world. This requires that you become a student of popular films, music, and books that most North Americans consume. This, however, does not mean that you do not challenge the "messages" of popular culture.

6. Make appointments to *listen* to outsiders. Go out with a neighbor or "unbeliever" in your church, not to evangelize, but

to *listen* to them. Interpret the "story beneath their story" and you will have an invaluable insight into where unchurched people really are coming from. There is no substitute for this. Often, the "how to's" of popular ministry books are woefully missing this. They are reporting on findings from the inside, not the outside. There are insights and hints of the way forward that you cannot find in practical ministry manuals, but only in deep understanding of people who live in your local community.

7. Frame your messages and conversations in such a way that Jesus and his gospel are the solution to *their desires*. Where is the overlap between all humans' desires and the truth of Jesus? What is beautiful about this message — that they wish it really was true? But show that the resources of Jesus are different than the path the world takes. Answer *their questions* with scriptural resources. Show them what they are in danger of truly losing without Jesus.

8. Understand that effective "translation" of Jesus and his gospel probably means that your ministry reaches a specific niche (psychographic). It is very difficult to be a missionary to several different cultures at the same time.

9. Emphasize the uniqueness of the person and work of Jesus that *cannot* be found anywhere else. Every university has people that are against war. Every secular family therapist emphasizes the importance of loving your family. What does Jesus offer that cannot be found anywhere else?

10. Think through your sermon with different kinds of people in mind: a 24-year-old, college skeptic; a 38-year-old, conservative, stay-at-home mom; a retired man with plenty of regrets, and so on.

11. Proclaiming a sermon centered on the human heart (motives) rather than one centered on the mind and/or moral action.

12. Speak with images and tangible metaphors rather than propositions.

13. Speak about existential realities rather than obligatory duties.

14. Don't simply talk about what happened in the Bible — but instead, what God is up to right now. (As if God is alive and active.)

29

Preaching To The Heart,
Not The Head

"Information" based sermons rarely bring about life change. This section explains the rationale and methodology of preaching to human motives.

"Our hearts are restless, until they can find rest in you."

-Augustine of Hippo

"You are what you love."

-James K. A. Smith

"Do not let your hearts be troubled. You believe in God; believe also in me."

-John 14:1

What Is The "Heart?"

-In the late modern world, we tend to think of ourselves as beings that primarily have *minds* (rational thoughts) and *bodies* with *feelings* or emotions. Therefore, today, preaching is primarily an act of *teaching* in-depth biblical content or it is *motivating* people through affective appeals. One could almost note the difference based upon denominations.

-Historically, Christian leaders believed that there is another key aspect of the human essence: the *"heart"* or the *"affections."* The heart is not merely our feelings. (Though that is often how we would refer to our emotions today.) Historically, the heart is the center of human life that loves, longs for, or desires *something*. For centuries, Christians maintained that if you truly want to know or understand a person, you must know or understand what they *love*. Many Christian bright-lights, through the history of the church, believed that our *heart* is the truest part of who we are.

-How our mind and emotions work reveal what our *heart* truly loves or desires. If an idea aligns with the pursuit of what we already love — we consider the idea to be a true or rational premise. If it is contrary to the desire of our affections — we believe it is in error or it is irrational.

-Similarly, if we believe that we are moving closer to achieving what are our heart is set upon, we *feel* happy or excited. If we believe that something is blocking us from having or possessing what our heart loves, we *feel* angry or depressed. (This of course reveals that our emotions are *not* simply *irrational*. Our emotional responses, whether positive or negative, are *revealers* of our deepest loves.)

The Heart Has Fallen Out Of Favor
-As the west became increasingly post-Christian, most people dropped the category of the human heart or the affections. If we are *only* biological beings, with rationally operating grey matter between our ears, we are *only* feelers and thinkers having nothing more than these sensations.

-Unaware of this philosophical shift on the nature of humanity, preaching has largely followed suit. Therefore, most contemporary preaching simply appeals to the head *or* to the feelings. (We teach more and more Bible information, *or* we try to motivate people to love God through inducing them to laughter or the shedding of tears.) However, if it is true that the human heart or affections is the "center" of a human person, well then, neglecting to preach to the heart leaves an individual "just as they were" before they encountered the sermon. Additionally, we can unintentionally, end up producing the next generation of Pharisees. We urge people to *believe* things, and to *do* things, or to *not do* things but they are not transformed in the depths of who they are. We have not entered (with the Spirit of Jesus) to their most defining core.

Preaching To The Heart
-Ask yourself questions such as: Why did the Holy Spirit include this text in the Bible? How does it deal with our deepest loves and desires? What does this passage or story reveal about what many people love or desire "beneath" the literal words of the text? What do we tend to love or trust other than the person of Jesus? How would loving and desiring Jesus (ultimately) satisfy our deepest self more than potential rivals? Why and how? Your answers to these kinds of questions may reveal how this passage deals with the human heart or affections.

-Imagine that you were counseling different individuals with a biblical text. How would you bring this to bear on their ultimate desires? On their ultimate struggles within a counseling context? How could you

31

make this real to them?

-Describe and illustrate palpably, why people trust in — what they trust in. Give plenty of examples that both show and explain these realities (not clichés — but how people actually live and what they, at very bottom, trust in and why.) Preaching to the heart is always dealing with the "thing that is underneath the thing that you are talking about" — it is lovingly, but kindly, naming the idols (both subtly and plainly). It is often dealing with why individuals continue to make "good things" into "ultimate" things.

-Illustrate and explain why placing our heart on these things — never quite satisfies, works, or brings the best out of human beings. At least, not in the long run....

Jesus As The Heart's Ultimate Fulfillment:

-Show how God, as revealed in Jesus Christ, offers a different kind of life, a life lived to the fullest (which obviously doesn't always mean happy life) when he is our ultimate desire.

-A preacher often needs to make use of metaphors that appeal to the five senses to make "heart" talk less abstract and more real. Use sensual images more than mere principles.

-Illustrate or give examples of how setting our affections on Christ plays out positively. (Again, this is not merely rational argument) but impressing the senses. This does not mean that everything simply "works out well" for the Christ follower but how a life based on Christ is truly better in a larger and more meaningful way. It is a more true, good, and *beautiful* life. But be careful, if we use Jesus as the ticket to "what works" our heart is not trusting in him. It is trusting in whatever "works." Which of course, eventually one day, won't work anymore.

-Give people some practical handles while being aware of the "sin of application." (Idol-making out of only *one specific way* to obey a scripture text instead of dealing with the heart and affections.) Multiple and varied practical handles should be offered.

How To Deepen Your Understanding Of The Human Heart:

-Read psychology — you will learn more about the inner workings and motivated strategies of human beings.

-Personally go through therapy or counseling — few things will teach you about the human heart like deep diving into your own.

-Read novels — writers excel at mining the insides of men and women.

-Deeply listen to "normal" people (particularly their words beneath their words beneath) — people are revealing insights about themselves all the time if you pay attention.

-Immerse yourself in historic, Christian spirituality — meditative prayer tends to reveal what and whom we truly love.

The (Open) Lord's Table

Fewer experiences are more meaningful to contemporary people than eating the body and drinking the blood of Christ. Suggestions are offered for making the most of this worshipful engagement.

[The Eucharist is] "the sacrifice of the cross perpetuated down the ages... This sacrifice is so decisive for the salvation of the human race that Jesus Christ offered it and returned to the Father only after he had left us a means of sharing in it as if we had been present there."

-Pope John Paul II

"Where we register that the material has become totally suffused by God, there alone we can be sure of material reality."

-Catherine Pickstock

"Whenever you eat this bread and drink this cup, you proclaim the Lord's death until he comes."

-1 Corinthians 11:26

-Take it as often as you can (weekly may be a bit much but not by much) — this tangible, tactile, expression of communion with Jesus — really connects with our culture of experience. We are an experience culture after all, not merely a thinking culture.

Prepping The Elements:
-Create an organized system for prepping the elements: where are items purchased from, who purchases them, and when do they know to do so? Create a schedule for those volunteers who will be prepping the elements and preparing the table up front as well as for those who will clean up afterward. Unwashed communion stuff gets nasty. You will need a pre-planned system of how many to prepare for — more than you think you'll need — nothing is worse than not having enough body of Christ available for people! Yes, this should be a volunteer activity, and not a staff activity... like nearly everything.
-Use a modified water bottle (angled squirt bottle) so that you do not

get wine/juice all over the place.

-You may want to consider always using gluten-free wafers. It's just easier that way.

-Take advantage of this opportunity, through all the little details, make this experience attractive for people who are just starting to connect with your church. Give some thought to the communion table (maybe a nice, black cloth?) possibly adorned with some local artist's iron crosses, a few candles (that look more like the old set of the MTV Unplugged concert series, than something from your grandmother's house), and so on. Thinking through all the little things to make a spiritual experience more meaningful is a large part of ministry.

-Often as you can, have people come up front to be served. It is much more participatory, you need to do everything you can to make worship more participatory. Remember Len Sweet's acronym: EPIC (experiential, participatory, image-centered, connective) as a helpful framework in designing worship experiences.

-Depending on your tradition, a great way to get other people involved in leading worship is to ask them to be the ones who physically serve the elements. (Always be thinking about how to get other people involved in meaningful ways.)

-First participants take the bread (someone says, "The body of Christ, broken for you.") Then they move to the wine (someone says, "The blood of Christ, shed for you.")

-Think through ahead of time where you will have people come up and then go back to their seats. You will need to give directions from up front. Nothing ruins a trip to the Lord's table like a foot traffic jam.

-Some churches are mixing up how they celebrate and take communion each time: coming up front and being served, passing them through the aisles, "self-serve" stations and the like.

Narrating And Delivering The Lord's Table:
-Increasingly, you are going to have to explain the actual purpose and meaning of communion. "This morning, we are going to celebrate the Lord's table, also known as communion. If you are new to our church, essentially, we are just going to walk up front and eat a piece of bread and drink some wine/grape juice. But to us followers of Jesus, this practice means so much more. On the night before Jesus was crucified, he ate a meal with his closest followers. He handed them bread and said to them: take, eat, this is my body. Then he shared the wine with them

saying: "Drink, this is my blood shared for you." I know this can sound kind of bizarre, but Jesus urged his followers to continually share this meal together to tangibly remind themselves how God, in Jesus, had his body beaten, and shed his blood on a cross, to demonstrate his undying love for all of us. We eat this bread, and drink this wine, to remember what Jesus did, to personally identity with Jesus.

If you are here this morning, and as best as you currently know how, you want to personally follow Jesus, you are welcome to celebrate communion with us today. Simply come down this far left aisle and then return down the center. However, if you are just not sure where you are personally with all of this God stuff right now, that's okay! We are so glad that you are here. Feel free to just hang out in your seat, someone will play some music, and we will continue with worship in just a moment…" [Prayer].

-Tie celebrating the Lord's table into an application of the sermon — as a way of responding to the message. Work hard at naturally framing it as an extension or conclusion to the message from the biblical text.

-Some traditions require people to be church members before they take communion, others require people to have a time of confession first, and others are just open to whomever is willing to receive from the table. Know your church, your tradition, and your personal opinion on these matters before you preside.

-Always have some live music playing while people take the elements. You may also want to scroll some select images on PowerPoint during this time.

Other Issues:

-Be sure to take communion to the infirm. This is very life-giving to recipients and is an important part of your duties. Read scripture to them. Ask them what they want prayer for. Pray for them (laying on of hands) and then take communion with them (reading the text of 1 Corinthians 11). Afterward, thank God for his love and his abiding presence in Christ.

-Don't rush the Lord's table or make it an unthoughtful add-on. It is too important of an experience for that.

-Depending on the person, their personality, and backstory, communion can be a "line-crossing" moment when they personally begin to trust Jesus. (Like the old sinners' prayer.) It may help to purposefully facilitate communion with this in mind, or at least, to take

36

note of who is participating for the first time.

-Many people are not big on children (who have not overtly come to faith) participating in communion. Personally, I do not understand this — but you must recognize many people feel this way.

-You will probably want to celebrate communion during the major Christian holidays: Christmas Eve, Palm Sunday, and Easter Sunday.

Meaningful Baptisms

Baptism is the classical initiation into the community of Christ. However, wise pastors leverage this rite into significant moments for all.

"We are saying, 'We are on this journey, this is our story, and it is now your story as well. And if you stick with us, we will help you live that story with us.' That's what baptism is all about."

-N.T. Wright

"The fact that baptism does the miraculous work of binding diverse flesh into one body means that baptism is one of the rites that effects the social salvation of humanity."

-Peter Leithart

"Go and make disciples of all nations, baptizing them in the name of the Father and of the Son and of the Holy Spirit."

-Matthew 28:19

Introductory Thoughts:
-If prepared thoroughly and thoughtfully, baptism can become not only a meaningful experience for the new believer, but also for their family members, the entire church, and even for unbelieving people. Certainly, you want this to be a genuine time of confessing sincere faith — however, your *secret job* as the pastor is to thoroughly *produce* this event (and all the required details) to make this an impactful experience for *everyone* present.

-Some people prefer baptizing people at the coast or in a river. Many perform baptisms during a special service on Sunday evenings. These have their advantages. But the advantage of baptizing during Sunday morning worship is that you will have the most witnesses possible and that this might be a meaningful God-experience for many beyond those who are being baptized.

Baptism "Evangelism":
-If you are ministering to college-educated adults, it may be rare for

them to naturally *volunteer* for baptism or any type of conversion-based experience. This will require you (or others) to not only evangelize people towards faith in Jesus, but possibly also to evangelize them towards baptism.

-Therefore, you will want to have baptism dates planned ahead of time on the calendar. You will want to purposefully and thoughtfully mount an overt and covert campaign to prepare people to be baptized. For example, preach about it in sermons, include decision cards as a response to a sermon, explain the importance in a newcomers' class, require it for membership, tap certain people to have private conversations and encourage people to consider baptism, and so on.

-Additionally, children's and youth directors/pastors should also be skillfully (yet certainly not manipulatively) encouraging the parents of children, and teens themselves, to consider baptism.

Preparing People For Baptism:
-Hand all people who are to be baptized (or their parents) an information sheet/packet about the purpose of baptism, information on self-evaluation, and a detailed step-by-step list of what they need to do and what will happen at the actual baptism service.

-Consider having all baptism candidates send you ahead of time (via email) their story of conversion and why they are being baptized. This will allow you to make sure they truly understand what they are doing. But additionally, you can edit their stories for length, and to make them more understandable for others who will attend the baptism. After editing, send it back to the candidate and make sure they are okay with it before moving forward. You don't want any surprises here.

-Determine who will baptize people: you, associate staff, and perhaps someone else. Depending on your tradition, you may leave it up to the one being baptized as to who they would like to baptize them. Many will choose you, but some may choose another family member or friend inside or outside of the church. This may make the experience even more meaningful for them.

-Consider coming up with a formal way for baptism candidates to invite family and friends (outside of the church) to attend the baptism. This is a great way to make new connections with people outside of faith. You can supply/help people make invitations, invite the family on stage, have a special reception for families afterward, or other similar ideas.

-You may want to ask the baptismal candidate if they want to read their story at their baptism or (if they are too nervous) have someone else read it for them. You may also want to consider having a picture of them on the screen when they are baptized.

-Provide in the packet, clear detailed directions for the candidate and/or their family:

-what time should they arrive? (Early enough to go over everything.)

-what should they wear? (Not white or sheer — something they can be immersed in, bringing a towel and change of clothes.)

-what are the details of the specific schedule? (A clear schedule of the entire service: musical worship, sermon, when they come up to the platform, when their story is read, when people pray, and the rest.)

-what exactly will happen? (How they will physically get in the tank, which microphones are used when they read their story, what the baptizer will say, the mode of baptism, and how they will physically get out of the tank.)

-Check with trustees about filling the tank, turning on the heaters, and other preparations that need to be made. Double-check to make sure this is being handled.

-Be sure that someone has secured and filled out baptism certificates ahead of time.

The Day Of Baptism:

-Meet the baptismal candidates well before the service and walk them through everything: where to be, what will happen, even slight demonstrations.

-Prepare a detailed list for yourself (and for the tech/sound people) as to who is being baptized, in what order, correct names, who is reading their story, when are prayers being offered, so that there are no questions about the service. The better this is planned out, the more meaningful it becomes.

-Go over details with sound people about mic/tech issues and safety.

"Kyle Lake, 33, pastor of University Baptist Church in Waco, Texas, died Sunday after being electrocuted while standing in the church baptismal during a morning service. Lake received a shock while adjusting a microphone before baptizing a woman. He was pronounced dead at 11:30 a.m. after being taken to the hospital. The woman being baptized was not yet in the water and was not seriously injured.

"At first, there was definitely confusion, just because everyone was trying to figure out what was going on," Ben Dudley, community pastor at University Baptist Church, told the Waco Tribune-Herald. "Everyone just immediately started praying." About 800 people were attending the service, which was more than usual due to Baylor University's homecoming weekend, reports the Associated Press." — Christianity Today

-Have someone quietly strum on the guitar or play the piano/keyboard during the baptism to create a meaningful atmosphere.

-Keep your comments (or whoever is baptizing them) brief. Just an introductory, *"We are so excited... Because this means..."* and that's it.

-Hold the hand of the candidate getting in the tank (you will want at least one other person there helping people to get in and out of the tank from the outside, and possibly, one other person in the tank to assist you with baptism). Have them take their time getting settled.

-Simply say their name, have them read their story (or someone read it for them) and then:

To candidate: Do you confess that Jesus Christ is your personal Savior and Lord; and are you willing to follow him in the fellowship of the church?

Candidate: I do.

Minister: On the confession of your faith I baptize you in the name of the Father, the Son, and the Holy Spirit. Amen.

-Have them hold their nose with one hand, place their other hand on that arm, and with your partner, dip them backward, and lift them back up. Clapping for them and/or laying hands on and praying for them afterward can be quite meaningful.

-Hold their hand as they get out; be sure they are handed a towel by the assistant outside the tank, and then they can walk away.

-You may want to video/take pictures of this. You can use it for promotional/annual meeting videos (if you get permission from them) and those being baptized may want to have a copy of the video for themselves.

-After you have baptized everyone, make an appeal or encouragement for others to consider following Jesus into baptism.

-Present the baptized persons with their baptism certificate afterward.

-Follow up with a handwritten note to those who were baptized and to their invited guests.

Dedicating Children,
Reaching Their Family And Friends

Gen Xers and millennials make parenting a massive priority. These desires can become strategic outreaches as well.

"All children... are 'gifts' to us. They are God's gifts not only to their parents, but also to the community, for they will grow up to be not only sons and daughters but also husbands, wives, friends, neighbors, and citizens."

-Marcia Bunge

"We lack a moral account of why we commit ourselves to having children... The family is morally crucial for our existence as the only means we have to bind time. Without the family, and the intergenerational ties involved, we have no way to know what it means to be historic beings. As a result we become determined by, rather than determining, our histories. Set out in the world with no family, without story of and for the self, we will simply be captured by the reigning ideologies of the day."

-Stanley Hauerwas

"Then people brought little children to Jesus for him to place his hands on them and pray for them. But the disciples rebuked them. Jesus said, 'Let the little children come to me, and do not hinder them, for the kingdom of heaven belongs to such as these.'"

-Matthew 19:13-14

The "Purpose" Of Child Dedications:

-A meaningful spiritual experience that helps people thank God for the gift of a child and that spiritually marks them in their role as a parent(s) and extended family (like a wedding ceremony). Meaning is often conferred through public rites and acts.

-In all honesty, child dedications *are* a Protestant replacement for infant baptism for churches that only encourage adult baptism. Be prepared, some may want to have a conversation about the potential meaning of child dedications: *is my baby going to heaven? Are they a Christian now? Will God specifically bless them because I have dedicated them to God?*

-Some (possibly many people) will be confused over the meaning or purpose of child dedication. Depending on your personality and theology, you may feel a need to help them understand the church's teaching before you consider performing the ceremony. Personally, I do *not* feel a need to do this. In my opinion, I believe that whatever people find meaningful and helps them to connect with God — I am all for. (Throughout church history, the clear majority of "normal people" have always been somewhat confused theologically. And yet, the Spirit has still moved within their lives!)

-Having a child dedicated will be very important to some families. (for example, if they have a Roman Catholic background, or something similar, they may throw a huge party around this). Other Jesus-loving people never feel the need to have their children formally dedicated to God.

-You will need to consider your own personal philosophy of who you will dedicate or not. Will it be only Christian families? Only church members? Anyone who asks for it?

-You may need to create a procedure for people to explore child dedication (like filling out a connecting card where people can sign up for a child dedication) or you can simply wait for people come to you. The direction you take will probably depend on how important or unimportant you believe that child dedications are. (How important or unimportant most people who live within your community believe that they are.)

Preparing For The Child Dedication:

-Plan the dedication with the family on the calendar *way* ahead of time. Encourage the parents to invite family and close friends and make the dedication a very big deal — you may even purchase/design invitations for them to send out to others. You may want to encourage them to host a lunch/party afterward. Do not waste this opportunity, it is a great way to connect with more people outside of the church. If handled with intentionality, you could see their close family and friends begin to attend your church after experiencing the child dedication. (After all, the gospel in the early church often spread "households.")

-Have the parents provide you with:

-The official full name of the child, what they informally call them, and their birthday. Also ask for the parents' formal names. (You may have them email them to you, so your spelling is correct. If you are unsure how to pronounce a name, please ask them!)

-Ask for a digital picture of the child that you can display on PowerPoint during the dedication. (A slide with the pic, full name of the child, and full name of the parents.)

-Gather info on any fun little details about their child: silly things they do, nicknames for him/her, any details that you can pepper in to the dedication.

-Get the names of any family members that will be at the child dedication and who they would like to have on stage with them. (Some may want to have other family members come up front — others do not.)

-Send the parents a detailed schedule a few days before the dedication and let them know when to arrive at church.

Sunday Of The Child Dedication:

-Greet the family and *generate* plenty of personal excitement for the event. It makes the day feel more meaningful for them. Physically lead them to exactly where they will stand on stage, how and where they will walk up, and other details. Go over the schedule with them in explicit detail. When they will come up front, they should know what exactly will happen, so that there is no confusion. Remind them that they do not have to say anything — only respond with *We will* when you ask them to. (Don't forget, public speaking is a huge fear for most people.)

-I would suggest that you only perform one child dedication a week (if possible) and *not* dedicate an entire group of families on the same Sunday. However, this is clearly not possible in a large church.

-Suggested order of the child dedication: (but of course — there are many ways to do this)

(Dedicate the child *after* the sermon)

-Call the family up to the stage. Have music playing quietly during this entire time — acoustic guitar or something similar, and have the child's picture up on the screen.

-Suggested liturgy: (but again, there are many ways to do this)

-*We praise and thank our Creator God for the gift of little*_____ *to _____ and _____. They are coming forward today desiring to publicly dedicate their son/daughter to our Lord Jesus Christ.*

-They are joined here today and supported by: _____ (mention family members and their roles) *and are thankful for the love and support they receive from their larger family and friends.*

-Little _____ was born on _____. He/she loves to _____ and _____. He/she makes her parents laugh when _____. What a joy and gift they are to their parents!

-Child dedication does not officially make a child a follower of Jesus. At some point, as this child grows and matures, they will need to make a personal decision to follow Jesus. But we dedicate children to our Creator: 1) To thank him for the gift of their lives... 2) To remind ourselves, that ultimately our children are God's and not our own... and 3) To commit ourselves, as parents and as a congregation, to serving and loving children in the ways of Jesus.

-(Have the congregation stand. This moves them past sitting passively and to actively engage) and then lead them in formal question and response:

-Do you _____ and _____ commit _____ to the God of our Lord Jesus Christ? Will you seek to prayerfully lead him/her in the ways of Jesus? If so, answer, "we will." (They respond.)

-Will you _____ and _____ trust the God of our Lord Jesus Christ with _____? Do you fully admit, that in the end, _____ is finally God's child and not yours? If so, answer, "we will." (They respond.)

-And you, congregation, will you commit to praying for _____ and _____ and little _____? Will you work to create a loving church community that aids _____ and _____ as they raise _____ in the ways of the Jesus? If so, answer, "we will." (They respond.)

-Place a small amount of olive oil in your hand (poured out from a decorative bottle) and place your hand on the child's forehead. Ask the congregation to extend their hands to the front and join in prayer. Then pray for the child, their parents, and the congregation. Afterward, quietly whisper to the family that they can go back to their seats.

-Applaud for the family as they leave the stage and encourage the congregation to meet them in the foyer after worship.

-After worship, be sure to go to the family (including extended family members) give them a hug, thank them for being there, and so on. If you are invited, be sure to attend lunch at their house or a restaurant afterward. This is a great way to meet and connect with people outside of the church. (Outreach often occurs through people's "networks" after all.)

Worship Teams, Tech Teams, And Staying Above The Drama

Many pastors find worship leaders and tech volunteers to be a hotbed for misunderstandings and personal conflicts. Advice on navigating this terrain is covered.

"Creative people alternate between imagination and fantasy, and a rooted sense of reality. Great art and great science involve a leap of imagination into a world that is different from the present. The rest of society often views these new ideas as fantasies without relevance to current reality."

-Mihaly Csikszentmihalyi

"The truly creative mind in any field is no more than this: A human creature born abnormally, inhumanly sensitive."

-Pearl S. Buck

"I appeal to you, brothers and sisters, in the name of our Lord Jesus Christ, that all of you agree with one another in what you say and that there be no divisions among you, but that you be perfectly united in mind and thought."

-1 Corinthians 1:10

Philosophy Of Public Worship
-Musical worship is *not* performing — it's creating a *context* where people can connect with God.
-When making decisions about the details of public worship, decisions should be made based on these priorities (in the following order):
1. What connects with "spiritually open" guests?
2. What the church regulars connect with?
3. What the worship team prefers?
4. What the worship leader likes?
-Look for as many ways as possible to make it participatory

and an actual *experience*. Participatory experience is the prevailing epistemology (way that people perceive truth) within out contemporary culture.

The "Ideal" Worship Leader

-At minimum, they must be a skilled musician and singer. They also need to be committed to Jesus and the church and have the ability to build a team.

-Ideally, they are also known for their spiritual depth, authenticity, artistic ability, and for their ability to connect with everyday people.

-Be wary of the talented, (but very young) worship leader who hasn't been "humbled" by life yet. Worship leading may become for them little more than their opportunity to perform.

-Keep in mind: even the "best" worship leaders often need administrative help. Artistic and detail work do not tend to come together in the same package.

Worship Leaders (And Their Teams)

-There are almost always "issues" with worship leaders and/or their teams. Worship leaders, by nature and temperament, are often performers and not shepherds. This is not anyone's fault; it is largely due to the fact that worship teams are creating collaborative art together. Tempers and egos and hurts are bound to surface.

-The main worship leader is the most visible person in the church other than the senior pastor. You want to keep them close to you. Being their very good friend (and the tech person's very good friend) is a real priority.

-To *somewhat*, stay ahead of conflicts, create a clear philosophy of worship that you regularly discuss with the worship leader, and once or twice a year, share with the entire worship team.

-Again, there *will be* personality conflicts on the worship team. To some degree, you must learn to roll with it. Conflict, in some form, will be inevitable. Do your best to avoid "triangles." Don't let people pull you in to take sides.

-Two other things: 1) Evaluate how helpful it for the worship leader to "talk" regularly during worship leading. Is there something specific that you would like them to say to the congregation? Or is it better for them to simply lead everyone musically? 2) Sometimes you need to step in and eliminate a song from their repertoire. This is rarely welcomed -

do it sparingly.

Tech Leaders

-Tech people tend to be rather "no-nonsense" types — very different from worship leaders. (This can create issues between them and the worship leader.) You may need to lead like a chameleon — be artsy with worship people and a "get 'er done" type with the tech leaders.

-Always respect the space of the tech people. You may need to instruct them on sound levels at times but don't touch anything! When you need to make a suggestion, do it respectfully.

-It is almost always worth investing money for tech leaders and worship leaders to go to seminars or to have expert coaches who work with them.

-Thank them all the time publicly — it goes a long way.

-Never take on worship leading or "tech stuff" yourself — you'll never be able to give it away. No one in a church ever stops the pastor from taking something on. You must be the one who looks out for this. If you never *learn* how to do it, you won't ever *have* to do it.

Which Style Or Genre Of Music?

-Many times, a great combination includes some classic hymns and some newer, soulful stuff all performed on contemporary instruments.

-High worship can "work" — but only for certain people groups.

-Boomers tend to value performance — younger adults tend to value stripped down and a sense of "authenticity" in worship. Whatever form worship takes, it must be *hopeful*. This is why people come to church.

-You may want to survey the congregation (including new unbelievers who attend) about what they resonate with — if there is a clear way forward — go with it. If people all over the map, keep things the way things have always been.

Need For Quality

-It is rarely enough to simply have a "nice" person lead worship. Especially if you want to reach outsiders. (New people are not moved by Aunt Sally's sincerity if she cannot sing well.) You need to have tryouts and a basic standard of acceptable musical and singing ability.

-However, you should have all kinds of different people on the worship team. Not *everyone* should be young or good looking!

-A decent budget for sound and tech equipment is often needed or worship can be rather distracting to worshippers and frustrating to those who serve on the team. But of course, you're not trying to offer a concert, you are rarely good enough for that. You are attempting to guide people into an experience with the Spirit.

Planning Sunday Worship

-Create a preaching schedule months out. Then you can meet with a creative team to brainstorm elements for worship and the worship leader has adequate time to plan out songs.

-Always listen to your worship leader but it's often best if the senior pastor has final say over the order and planning of worship. (That doesn't mean planning out individual songs.) It's the main event of the church where you connect with most people — don't give this away.

-You need a bit of variety in Sunday worship but it helps to have a general pattern. (For example: unbelievers often skip the musical worship portion on purpose. They will be angry if you move this around.)

-BTW — if your church is lacking musicians and vocalists — it's likely because the church takes too much of a *rational approach* to spirituality. If the church is more open to mystery, the human condition, and the surprising movements of God, you likely won't lack for all kinds of artists.

Handling Leadership

Leading Staff So That They
(More Than) Like You

Young pastors tend to be quite friendly with staff. This section offers what they tend to struggle with: leading and managing their staff for effectiveness.

"Leaders will follow you not because of your position or charisma but because they consider it in their interest. Your job as a leader is to convince them that their interests lie with you."

-Jeswald Salacuse

"Having a bad manager is often a one-two punch: Employees feel miserable while at work, and that misery follows them home, compounding their stress and negatively affecting their overall well-being."

-Jim Harter

"The things you have heard me say in the presence of many witnesses entrust to reliable people who will also be qualified to teach others."

-2 Timothy 2:2

Before You Hire:

-Create a very clear job description ahead of time. Know what *specific* skills the new staff member needs to possess. (They will *not* possess *all* skills) . Looking for a "well-rounded and complete" person is a surefire guarantee that the search process will not go well. A strength in one area, becomes a weakness in another. Know what *specifically* you need from this person and just as important, what you *don't* need from them.) Two or three primary skills are usually sufficient. A children's ministry director likely needs to be organized, able to recruit volunteers, and work with a team. They do not necessarily need to be theologically educated, off-the chart extroverts, amazing public speakers.

-In consultation with your church board, calculate potential salary and benefit costs to determine if a hire is possible. (Few churches have all the money on hand for a new hire. However, it should be *reasonably* possible.)

-Some pastors believe that they should get final say on whom to hire. Other churches make the decision through a vote of the church board or even entire congregation.

Who To Hire:

-Do *not* hire people based simply on aspirations; hire people based on their *proven* skills, personality, and way of being. The adage is a true one: *the best predictor of future behavior is past behavior.*

-Always hire people who are different from you (different skills and personality) but with similar values and philosophy of ministry.

-In general, good hires are people who: 1) Are "leaders of leaders" — they have a high ceiling and can *reproduce* themselves *and* 2) Those who have already been "broken" — people who have hit bottom and have bounced back. "Leaders of leaders" will be able to grow, develop, and build a ministry. ("Doers" do not do this.) People who have been "broken" tend to exude a spirit of grace and maturity. People who have not been broken, will eventually, break themselves *and* others.

-Increasingly churches are hiring part-time staff. Hiring from among their committed volunteers, they are assured of the skills and values of the new employee. (They already know their skills and that they fit the vision of the church *and* the senior pastor.) Additionally, part-time staff member allows the church to leverage an individual's gifting without having to pay for benefits and give them more assignments (to fill their time) that they may not be most suited for.

-However, if you are hiring someone who must have trained ministry skills: preaching, teaching, or executive leadership, you may need to conduct a more national search.

Hiring Process:

-Design a solid job placement ad: job description, skills needed, church values, and other similar desires. If this is written specifically and not generically, you will attract more of the right kind of candidates. List it online, send it to friends, and others.

-Search steps:

    1. Candidate sends in a resume.

    2. After sorting through them, narrow it down to maybe eight or ten and email them asking them to answer some open-

ended, essay questions. (This helps you to discern fit for your church's culture.)

3. Pick 3 to 5 to interview (via vvideo conference) and when down to 2 or 3, in-person. (By the in-person interview stage, check all the references and run a legal background check.)

4. Offer someone the position (give them a week to decide to accept it or not.)

-Increasingly, churches are using outside hiring agencies to conduct the searches for them. (These are not cheap — around half of a year's salary.) However, many times they offer to complete a second search for free *if* the person you hire leaves within a short time.

After You Hire Someone:

-Facilitate purposeful training and orientation for a new staff member: budget and how to access funds, keys and locks, legal policies and procedures, specific church philosophies, and other important details.

-Meet with them one-on-one, possibly daily, for the first week to help get them going.

-Identify some lay-people in the church who will purposefully serve as their pseudo-parents and/or buddies within the church. (They are going to need an emotional/relational support system beyond you.)

-No matter how much due diligence you invest — the new hire will *always* be somewhat different from what you expected. The wise church leader will then *adjust* the job description to fit their natural gifts and abilities. The art of managing well is putting people in a position where they can use their God-given gifts and abilities to assist the church.

Managing And Relating To Staff:

-They must know that you *know* them: personally, their spouse, their background, and more. You should be closer to them than nearly everyone else in the church. However, they cannot be your best friend. You do have to lead them after all.

-Have them over as a family now and then.

-At least weekly, there should be light/fun interaction with staff.

-You are the chief caregiver for any staff member in case of emergencies or struggle.

-Meet with them weekly (or every other week) to: problem shoot for them, resource them, coach them, help leverage their gifts for the church, go over very clear goals and expectations, and to pray with them and for them.

-Make available ongoing training and development for them. (Pay for them to attend seminars, have an outside coach, or something similar.)

-Be sure you speak well of them publicly and "have their back" when people complain about them.

-In general, they should be *self*-motivated. If *you* must motivate them and let them know *exactly* what they should do — they should not be paid staff. People who are worthy of a staff position are the type of people who primarily only need you to cast a larger vision and then get out of the way.

Facilitating Staff Meetings:

-Weekly staff meetings are a must for any well-run, well-managed, focused ministry. Even if the church does not have many paid staff members, or full-time staff members, it is still possible to facilitate weekly (or at least monthly) staff meetings.

-Staff meetings are essential to: review and evaluate the most recent programming and events of the ministry, to discuss and coordinate over pressing issues and upcoming events, to troubleshoot and assign various ministry tasks and administrative assignments, and to make sure that all people who oversee and facilitate various ministries of the church are on the same page.

-Ideally, anyone who oversees any ministry or task of the church: children, youth, worship, facilities, administration, outreach, community service, tech, and finances, are all present. (Larger churches often hold these weekly, often on Tuesday mornings, where all paid staff are present. Smaller churches may hold these monthly, where all key volunteer overseers of different ministries are present.)

-Staff meetings are altogether different than board meetings: board meetings are intended to focus on "big-picture" vision, strategy, and legal matters, while staff meetings should focus on smaller, day to day, running of the details of the ministry matters. To confuse these two, is to often guarantee that the ministry does not operate very effectively. People who actually carry out the work of the ministry (staff) should pay attention to the implementation of ministry goals while the church board should focus on larger matters, such as entire church goals for the next year or two, staff meetings should focus on implementation and daily matters such as why it took so long to check in children to their class last Sunday, and so on.

-Ideal staff meeting schedule:

    -senior leader welcomes participants and thanks them for their ministries

    -Checking in/hearing about any noteworthy personal events/ needs. (birth of a child, birthdays, new roles)

    -Vision-casting/training as needed. (sharing about big-picture plans, reviewing important articles that may be relevant, reviewing a book together)

    -Asking each leader to (briefly) share what is going on in their current ministry (positively and negatively) so that everyone is on the same page and possibly, so that one staff member may offer a solution for another one.

    -Reviewing any details that are needed for whole staff coordination. (planning for Christmas Eve worship, or adding a new worship service)

    -Praying all together.

-Be sure to not allow the meeting that is intended to cover matters that are germane to all staff members to devolve into a lengthy discussion that only involves a couple of staff members. If prolonged conversation is needed, and it does not involve everyone, ask the participants to quickly make plans for another private meeting to discuss these matters instead of needlessly wasting everyone else's time.

Firing Staff:

-Be sure to check with your attorney and discuss this matter as a board, before proceeding.

-A staff member should almost never be *surprised* if they get let go: you should have had clear goals for them, and they should have known for some time, that they are not meeting them, they should have been engaged in several conversations regarding their performance, have been sent for additional training and coaching, ongoing issues were documented, before anyone is terminated.

-If they are terminated over a moral issue — it must happen *quickly*. If it is a "competency or job fit" issue — it takes much longer. Basically, you need to wait until many volunteers who work with them are threatening to quit unless they are removed. That it has become rather evident that this is not working.

-Once it is clear that termination is needed, do it quickly and immediately.

-No matter the reason, you will take a serious hit for this — be sure that it was essential. The "upside" for the whole ministry must be much greater than the "downside" you will personally experience.

-Provide a gracious package for them on the way out. Assign a board member to be their liaison regarding any possible stipulations.

-Be sure to notify other staff members before it gets out publicly.

-Consult with an attorney first, but you may need to provide a reason for the termination to the entire congregation. People will talk either way.

Board Meetings That Move
The Mission Forward

Every pastor has a church board, few pastors know how to relate to them and cultivate them for what matters. This entry offers an overview of board dynamics.

"There is one thing all boards have in common, regardless of their legal position. They do not function. The decline of the board is a universal phenomenon of this century."

-Peter Drucker

"When the topic of leadership is brought up, we tend to immediately begin talking about how to lead 'doers.' Leading other leaders is, in many ways, different than leading doers. Leaders expect you to interact with them differently."

-Timothy Parsons

"The apostles and elders met to consider this question."

-Acts 15:6

Purpose Of A Church Board:
-Church boards exist for two reasons: 1) They are the legally responsible officers who preside over a non-profit corporation. They are, quite literally, liable for the financial and legal decisions of the church. 2) They are the "spiritual overseers" of a local ministry. Typically, both kinds of matters are covered in a board meeting.

Characteristics of ideal Church Board Members:
1. Personal commitment to Jesus.
2. Personal commitment to the local church. However, talented leaders won't always be at every event. Be careful to not assume that "commitment to the church" equals participating in all church events. If someone is a natural leader with real ability, they will often travel quite a bit for work and be involved with multiple organizations. Do not pass over them as a potential board member because they are not

61

always around. You could end up cutting the church off from some needed perspectives and gifts that they have to offer.

3. Natural (or spiritually gifted) executive ability. They are big picture people who can easily consider matters as they play out for the *entire ministry*. They are strategic leaders, who intuitively understand how organizations and communities operate. They think about what is best for the entire church and not simply what matters to them personally.
4. Someone who is not necessarily your biggest fan or harshest critic. They will speak the truth.
5. Has a different perspective, personality, or background from others who are currently on the board.
6. Likely should not include other pastoral staff members (except for the senior pastor and the executive pastor.)

There is a massive difference between a healthy and unhealthy church board. Who serves on the board can literally make or break the church. Choose members carefully and prayerfully!

Possible Schedule of a Board Meeting:

- Welcome and Prayer
- Scripture Meditation
- Discussing an article? Book chapter?
- Agenda Items
- Closing Prayer

Elements That Make A Board Meeting Work:
-Send meeting agendas out a minimum of a week ahead of time. Sensitive matters that involve specific individuals should likely be kept off agendas or recorded very vaguely.

-Board meetings are held no more frequently than once a month and maintain a strict time schedule. If there isn't anything that needs to be discussed- cancel the meeting.

-Provide coffee, donuts, or other treats for those who are on the board. You want them to enjoy the meeting as much as possible! It does *not* have to be a dry, stuffy, formal meeting.

-Only discussing "big-picture" and complex matters — avoiding decisions that micro-manage or that are best left to the staff. Agenda items should include: legal and/or financial matters; hiring, evaluating, and terminating of staff; creating a vision, goals, and strategic plans (and evaluating them); dealing with thorny ethical/moral issues and policies. (In general, matters that staff should not ethically decide by themselves or that are too complex for staff to decide on their own.) Decisions such as: what should be the topic of our next sermon series, evaluating that new song that was sung in worship, how to create a check-in system for children's ministry that works, etc. should be staff decisions and not board decisions.

-Everyone shares openly and honestly. (They serve the church by having to wade into difficult matters that most people don't want to bother with. Therefore, to make solid and helpful decisions, people need to feel free to share openly and honestly — knowing that the conversation will remain in confidence.)

-People feel free to openly and kindly disagree with each other. You are not dealing thoroughly with matters and creating helpful decisions if people are not disagreeing with each other.

-Someone must keep notes on the meeting for legal purposes. These are to be made available in the church files and for other members to read. (Notes do not record all the *discussion*. Only *decisions*. Some extremely sensitive matters, such as pertaining to a specific individual, should be left out of the notes.)

Pastor's Role In Board Meetings (Assuming you are the board chair):

-The goal is to facilitate a conversation and decision-making. You want everyone to share and ward off the "bullies" who want to dominate meetings. If someone is not speaking up, directly ask them for their opinion. If someone is dominating conversation, ask them to allow others to share.

-Name the general pattern that you hear emerging from the conversation and how bits and pieces from various perspectives could possibly coalesce into a helpful decision.

-Affirm comments that you think are particularly helpful or insightful.

-Ask questions that you believe people may not be considering.

-Stand firm (while maintaining a pastoral posture) on your beliefs and key values and mission for the church. But remain *very* flexible on *how* people choose to specifically implement them.

-Consensus is a poor goal but don't make a major decision if the board is divided.

-Use the church board as your litmus test for what the Spirit of God is up to. Sometimes you have an idea but the board isn't for it. This could be because: 1) You are wrong. 2) You are right- but the church isn't ready. 3) You are right but this is wrong for this specific church.

Relating To Board Members:

-The wise pastor will work at personally being close to board members. If they are in trouble, you should personally minister to them. Other than your staff, you should be closer to board members than anyone else in the church. It might sound strange, but part of their "pay" is getting to hang out with you.

-At minimum, the board should do something fun together at least once a year.

-Regularly hang out with your board members- especially the tough ones. If you stay close to surly board members, you are a little more likely to gain them as an ally (they will give you the benefit of the doubt if you have a positive relationship with them) and they will never surprise you in a meeting. You will know, ahead of time, where they stand on various issues.

Seeing With An Outsider's Eyes

Too many pastors, even millennial pastors, only preach to the choir. Here, tips on learning to see the church like the unchurched do is offered to the reader.

"Why do we engage in community analysis? The simple answer is so that we may bring about peace, harmony, welfare, and fullness to those around us. Because that is what God calls us to do."

-John Fuder

"If you aren't smelling awful smells sometimes, then you're not where Jesus is."

-Leonard Sweet

"When evening comes, you say, 'It will be fair weather, for the sky is red,' and in the morning, 'Today it will be stormy, for the sky is red and overcast.' You know how to interpret the appearance of the sky, but you cannot interpret the signs of the times."

-Matthew 16:2-3

The Essential Need To Understand The Local Culture:
-There is no such thing as a "culture-less" Christianity — faith always incarnates within a specific culture.

-People often only personally find Christ *within* their own culture. The gospel of Jesus must be similar enough to connect with people — and yet different enough to bring challenge. If the gospel takes a form that is too alien to their own culture, it does not seem plausible or enticing.

-Importing your own personal brand of "enculturated Christianity" to a church or local community is not helpful, effective, or loving. Ministry isn't about doing church in a way that *you* personally enjoy. But what is helpful for *these* people, who live within *this* place and culture.

-Watch out for books and ministry seminars that trick you into importing an alien form of enculturated faith to a location where it doesn't fit.

How To Understand The Local Culture (this will take real intentionality):

-Research the history. The "reason" that a place was formed never completely leaves the ethos of the city, town, or nation.

-Research demographic changes — they will cue you in to where things are going.

-Listen to locals on how they describe their town or city. You can pick up important clues from doing this but you have to learn to interpret their comments and not simply take them at face value.

-Notice the design of architecture: buildings, roads, neighborhoods. It says a lot about local values. The largest buildings in town represent the highest values of the locality.

-What do these people do for fun?

-How does this town or city compare/contrast with other ones?

-What are the greatest strengths of the community? Where do their values align with the vision of Jesus? (Use these to connect with people.)

-What are the greatest needs of the community? Where do their values run contrary to the vision of Jesus? (This is where you have something "different" to offer people.)

-Remember: in every locale there is a counter-culture (a smaller group that has different values and narratives than the dominant local culture). Some churches find very fruitful ministry by intentionally building bridges with these communities.

Thinking Through Your Church With Outsider Eyes:

-Remember, most new people are quite anxious about showing up to your church for the first time. They are afraid they will be asked to do something weird, they will be embarrassed, they will be pointed out, or that the whole experience will just be an irrelevant waste of time.

-They have no idea where to go or what to do. Are there adequate signs guiding them along? Are there greeters explaining where to take their children? Are there people showing them where to get coffee, or any other items?

-They may not know what any of your words mean: fellowship, atonement, liturgy, catechism, saved, Eucharist. Think through all your language and explain what these words mean — every Sunday.

-Explain the *hows* and *whys* of all experiences and practices. Admit, that it may feel weird at first, but that it's okay.

-Always assume that there are people present on Sunday who do not believe and who are somewhat skeptical about faith and the Bible. (And if you assume this, and handle things accordingly, it is much more likely that they will show up.)

Elements That "Naturally" Connect With Outsiders:

-Friendly people who casually seek them out.

-Music, pop-culture elements, attire, and more that seems to fit their culture. It communicates that you understand them.

-A narrative spirit that leads toward finding personal freedom and a life of meaning. (As opposed to finding forgiveness and righteousness — these are insider, religious values.)

-A genuinely spiritual atmosphere. Otherwise, why would they be there?

-Sermons that combine the biblical story with their story. Sermons that are meaningful and honest and include challenging elements without attacking anyone.

-Sermons that deal with everyday life issues: job/career, relationships, money, personal struggles, finding a sense of purpose, overcoming hurts, forgiveness issues, and so on. (This doesn't mean these need to be topical sermons. But these are the issues that tend to interest everyday people.)

Strategic Planning For The Kingdom

Pastoral ministry is certainly a busy affair. A basic understanding of the practical dimensions of strategic planning can help the church leader to focus efforts on what truly matters.

"It is meaningless to speak of short-range and long-range plans. There are plans that lead to action today... they are true plans, true strategic decisions. And there are plans that talk about action tomorrow — they are dreams... pretexts for nonthinking, nonplanning, nondoing."

-Peter Drucker

"Strategy is about making choices, trade-offs; it's about deliberately choosing to be different."

-Michael Porter

"I have become all things to all people so that by all possible means I might save some. I do all this for the sake of the gospel, that I may share in its blessings."

-1 Corinthians 9:22-23

Purpose:
-It is essential for any organization, community, or mission to create a specific *strategic* plan. To be effective at *anything* is a matter of "focus" and purposefully choosing to neglect the myriad of positive activities that a church *could* do but will strategically choose *not* to do. An attempt at "being everything" is choosing to be "nothing." This is can be a real difficulty for well-meaning church leaders, who struggle to say "no" to any possibility.

-Strategic plans have a way of fostering proper confidence. Donors and leaders increase their faith in the church: *"We are being led well. People actually have a plan and they know what they are doing."* Often, a reasonable strategic plan will need to be in place before high-capacity people feel comfortable investing time and money into the ministry. But strategic plans also foster healthy confidence within the pastor's being

68

— the plans cut through the vast clutter of possibilities and help make it very clear what the church and her resources should specifically focus on.

The Importance Of Understanding Organizational Identity:

-Many over-emphasize "vision" and miss the crucial element of "identity" which every thriving organization and communication must make clear.

-There are all kinds of churches. And the *kingdom* needs all kinds of churches to reach all kinds of different people. However, the *only* reason for a *specific* church to exist is if she is doing something different, with a slightly different communal DNA, than all the other churches within the local community. If another church is already doing "so and so..." or already has the culture of "so and so..." this particular church truly does not need to exist. It should close shop and go join the other one!

-In prayerfully discerning the identity of a church, it can be helpful to consider:

1. Who are the people who make up this church? What are they already excited about? (As opposed to trying to motivate them to be excited about.)

2. Who is the pastor of this church? What are his/her God-given gifts and passions?

3. What makes this church unique compared to other local ministries?

4. What about this church could connect with, and be meaningful to, people outside of faith in Jesus?

-Thriving organizations and ministries doggedly hold on to their values and their "spiritual DNA" but they are willing to try and experiment with new strategic tactics all the time. Slowly dying ministries assume that strategic tactics are the same as values and "spiritual DNA" and thus become rigid and slowly irrelevant. Floundering ministries are constantly moving this way and that way, consistently questioning their values and "spiritual DNA" and thus having no specific identity at all. And without an identity there is not much life.

-If the church does not have a clear identity, use the practice of church survey (or appreciative inquiry) listed below to gain some "data." Then seek to prayerfully discern the findings and create a possible identity that seems to fit the church. Finally, work it through it (allowing their edits) with your board and staff team.

Creating And Facilitating A Church Survey:

-"Surprise" people during a couple of Sunday mornings with personal surveys for them to complete. (Quite literally have them fill out the survey during the worship gathering. This assures a large amount of participation.) The value of personal surveys (instead of group discussions) is that *way* more people, will be *way* more honest. In a group discussion, the loudest voices tend to take over and skew your impressions of the opinions and inclinations of much of the congregation.

-Questions *can* and *should* involve:

-Demographic elements: gender, age, marital status, how long they have been a part of the church, how they self-define themselves spiritually, and similar questions.

-First impression elements: *How did they first hear about the church? What led them to check it out for the first time? What was their first impression of the church? What did they like? What did they not like or not understand? If they had previously been a part of another church, how do they feel that this church is similar or dissimilar to previous experiences?*

-Identity and effectiveness elements: *How has your life changed or remained the same since joining this church? What are the top three things that you appreciate about this church? What are your top three suggestions for how this church could improve? What is one significant obstacle to your non-churchgoing friends checking out this church? What phrase would you use to describe this church to a friend?*

-Collate the responses you received into one document — looking for clear patterns (even if people frequently use different words in their descriptions, themes tend to become rather clear.).

-Knowing where the church is (and assuming you reasonably understand yourself and the local community) prayerfully sit down and attempt to discern the values and specific identity of your church. Give a copy of the survey results, and your attempt to describe a church identity, to members of your church board and staff. Let them suggest edits, with the church board granting final approval.

Strategic Planning Meeting With The Church Board:

-Spend adequate time in prayer and meditation before organizational planning begins.

-Hand all members a copy of the summarized survey data, the church values and identity statements, and ask them to individually, and prayerfully, consider the present state of the church and what should be the main five primary goals for the next two years. (Remind them that their role is to not to push for *their* personal preferences, but what they believe is best for the church as a *whole*.) Give them ample time alone to write down five goals privately, without discussion. (Again, this keeps one persuasively personality from swaying everyone.)

-Afterwards, ask the board to brianstorm tactics for achieving these five. Write them on a white board. As everyone shares, look for similarities and try to whittle their feedback down to five goals. If there are more than five that stand out, have people *privately* vote on them (in order of preference) and pick the five that end up with the most votes. (Having any more than five main goals is having too many goals.)

-After you have settled on five goals for the church, ask the board to brainstorm strategies and tactics for these five goals. (Specific *action* steps that you will use to try achieving these goals.) Write everything down, but remind the board, that these specific tactics will need church *staff* input — since they are the ones charged with carrying out the implementation of these goals.

Final Elements:
-Take the five goals and suggested tactics to the church staff. Allow them ample time to brainstorm additional tactics and to remove specific suggestions that the church board generated.

-In a separate meeting, for each tactic, assign a staff person or key leader to be the "one" person responsible for this initiative and list a date when it is to be completed by.

-Take this strategic plan back to the church board for final approval.

-As time goes on, review the strategic plan and its implementation with the board at each monthly meeting. The pastor and board should be open to possible *revisions* according to the results (or lack thereof) of the strategic plan. The five goals, most of the time, should *not* be changed over the next two years. However, specific tactical strategies of implementing them should be open to revision based on new possibilities, challenges, and the results on the ground.

-Share the plan with the church at the annual meeting/vision night. Main emphasis should be on the church identity and values and five goals for the next two years. However, specific strategic tactics may be shared. (But its likely wise to only list some "highlighted" specific strategies and not to mire in the weeds when sharing these publicly.)

Example Of A Goal And Specific Tactical Strategies:

Goal: First Fresno Church will be in a financially healthy position that creates a sense of stability and security and that provides the resources to advance kingdom ministry.

Strategy	Responsible Point Person	Completion Date
1. 6-Week Sermon Series on Giving	Pastor Jose	4/21
2. Lead members in making an annual giving commitment. Mail them bi-annual updates of their commitments.	Jane Smith	9/21
3. Have "regular people" from the church share their personal story(on a monthly basis) of why they financially invest in the church during Sunday worship.	Pastor Jose	(Begin 12/20)
4. Snail mail a financial letter to all church members- complete with church vision and strategies AND with a detailed budget for the next year.	Pastor Jose/Jane Smith	1/14/21
5. Highlight (monthly during Sunday worship) Stories of what the church is doing within the local community.	Assoc. Pastor Maria	1/20
6. List a monthly updated financial status of the church within the emailed prayer guide.	Edna Taylor	12/14/20
7. Redesign the offering envelopes and include with each of them detailed info on how to simply participate in direct deposit.	Jane Smith	12/20/20
8. Investigate using text-based giving smart phone apps and create a proposal as to how we could utilize them.	Curt Santiago	2/1/21
9. Complete a thorough review of the current budget and propose if there is anything that should be cut out and/or streamlined.	Tony Sosa	3/10/21

| 10. Create a database and propose a specific strategy for reaching out to foundations and notable wealthy individuals who may be interested in giving towards specific outreach initiatives within the local church. | Pastor Jose/ Assoc. Pastor Maria | 2/1/21 |

Creating Church Calendars,
So You Don't Create A Mess

Planning goes a long way to keeping everything from falling apart. Specific processes are necessary though, to create a calendar that involves multiple constituencies and ministries.

"Sentimentality plays with sweet intentions in place of good sense."

-Jane Jacobs

"It does not do to leave a live dragon out of your calculations, if you live near him."

-J.R. R. Tolkien

"Why, you do not even know what will happen tomorrow. What is your life? You are a mist that appears for a little while and then vanishes. Instead, you ought to say, 'If it is the Lord's will, we will live and do this or that.'"

-James 4:14-15

Why Are We Even Spending Time On This?
-Ministry in general, and kingdom work in particular, is hard enough (because you are working against the natural desires of many people) that you don't need to make it more difficult for people to join in because everything is thrown together at the last minute, or because people already had other meetings scheduled due to your calendar not being scheduled far enough ahead.

-Serious calendar planning keeps you from offering too many church activities or too little. Too many activities wear people out, lessens your voice, and creates a culture of mediocrity. Too few activities limit real community and momentum building.

-There are only so many "time slots" available. Calendar planning forces you to hone in on your true values and priorities.

-Calendar planning will lessen friction between staff members and key volunteers and ease the stress they experience as individuals. They are giving a lot - you want to make their job as easy as possible.

-Those few, but really organized and "go-getter" types will appreciate that you are getting a calendar out early. (And you *want* them to like you.) People with skills, options, and professional jobs — do nothing last minute. Churches should plan a minimum of six months out. Large churches may plan up to two years out.

-You likely need to have the church calendar completed before other people can book or rent the church facility.

-You can (within reason) plan the schedule around *your* schedule. This may be a nice little perk that you can utilize.

Working On The Calendar *Before* The Team Meets To Work On The Calendar

-Gather calendars from local school districts and make note of: three-day weekends, spring break, the big football game, and other details. You don't want to create church events that compete with these. (Not to mention a general "holiday" calendar.)

-Have staff members come to your planning meeting having already done their work: a list of possible events/dates for their various ministries, plus other events.

-Programming elements that you will likely need on a calendar: Sunday Public Worship (and guard it), small groups/fellowship groups, social justice/neighborhood service, outreach/evangelism events, and deeper spirituality/growth classes.

A Few Things To Keep In Mind Before Working On The Calendar With Your Team

-You must think through what is best for the "whole church" and know your priorities ahead of time… There are only so many possible "whole church" events - you cannot make *everything* a priority.

-If you pastor a smaller church (500 or fewer people) work very hard to prevent different church events from competing with each other (being held at the same time). Larger churches cannot avoid this- but they do want to be mindful of "whole church" events. (In general, smaller churches expect that everyone should be at everything — larger churches expect certain people will be at certain activities and other people will be at other ones. This is one of the differences between a larger church and a smaller one.)

-You will need to give attention to the church and neighborhood culture in order to plan and schedule activities appropriately. Churches filled with professionals — can rarely organize anything during the week (except possibly, high-commitment, discipleship oriented stuff). Other churches, primarily consisting of working class folk, often long for midweek activities. The church is a lifeline for them.

-In general, stay away from Saturday evening events. (Unless you don't want people to show up on Sunday.) Very few people will make it a point to attend church twice in one weekend.

-As a rule of thumb, these are your limits for "whole church" events: maybe one, at most, two weeks of special projects during a calendar year. (An all hands-on-deck VBS week, "Serve the City Week" and so on). In addition, you can likely schedule only three other "special one-day events" during the same calendar year in which you are trying to get everyone to be there.

Working On The Calendar With Your Team

-Quite literally bring several blank calendars to your staff calendar planning meeting.

-Begin by scheduling what the "whole church" needs. (You may also have to explain *why* this is the case.)

-After you have scheduled the "whole church" events — sub-ministries begin to share their preferences and you serve as the facilitator in helping to bring healthy balance to the scheduling. Pencil things in. Begin negotiating, working everything through, thoroughly.

-You may have to arbitrate who gets first say — to what and why. This is an art form. You need to be fair, but also, keep in mind what is best for the whole church during this season.

-Only a few activities ever get the prime spots. I suggest that you give these to outreach events. (You are always pumping water uphill on outreach as it is.)

Getting The Calendar Out To The People

-Be sure to give a special copy to trustees, staff, and others who consistently deal with the facility.

-You do have to plug things like crazy today before anything begins to register with people. But you cannot truly "push" everything — only very small churches can do this. You can likely only "push" one event at a time.

-Hand out calendars during two straight Sunday mornings, snail mail them to all regular attendees, promote events on social media sites, church emails, website, and the like. The more ways that you can get it out there, the better.

People Won't Trust You If You Can't Manage A Budget

Creating and managing budgets are necessary skills that few younger pastors possess. Knowing budgeting is essential to gaining respect and keeping failure at bay.

"The early Christians were communists, as the book of Acts quite explicitly states... the first converts in Jerusalem after the resurrection, as the price of becoming Christians, sold all their property and possessions and distributed the proceeds to those in need, and then fed themselves by sharing their resources in common meals... To be a follower of the Way was to renounce every claim to private property and to consent to communal ownership of everything."

-David Bentley Hart

"Stewardship involves moving from patriarchy to partnership and from security to adventure. To achieve this leaders must... build widespread financial accountability throughout the organization."

-Peter Block

"As Jesus looked up, he saw the rich putting their gifts into the temple treasury. He also saw a poor widow put in two very small copper coins. "Truly I tell you," he said, "this poor widow has put in more than all the others. All these people gave their gifts out of their wealth; but she out of her poverty put in all she had to live on."

-Luke 21:1-4

-A budget is a goal or a guide for a congregation, it's never exact- life doesn't *quite* work according to budgets. However, you need to stick to agreed upon budgets as much as possible. This will either gain you respect (you will be viewed as a competent leader/manager) or it will undercut your ministry.

Staff Members And Budgets:
-A helpful approach is to use zero-sum budgeting. (This is building

78

the budget from scratch each year rather than taking what was and simply adding to it or trimming it.) This cuts down on wasteful spending and avoids creating a culture where people guard their budgets (even if they do not need the funds this year) for fear of having them slashed.

-Assuming the church budget covers a calendar year (rather than a fiscal year) — it may be helpful to have all staff members and/or lay-leaders who oversee various line items on the budget — to bring their budgets to a meeting in either August or September. Their proposed and detailed budgets should include: essentials, real needs, and *wishes* all of which are labeled accordingly. (This means that *every* ministry needs to do long-range planning.) The easiest way for each person to prepare their budget is to look over detailed expenditures from the previous year. (Not the previous year's budget — but actual *expenditures*.) As well as reviewing the strategic plan for their ministry over the next year and creating detailed estimates.

-Go over the budgets together, offering counsel, and adjusting accordingly. When completed though, be sure to remind staff members that their budget is not yet set it stone. There will be more iterations that it will have to go through.

Building A Master Budget:

-Combine the budgets from the various ministries into a master budget sheet (broken down into sub-categories) and then check out the final, overall budget total.

-At minimum, your board will need to approve the final budget (and possibly the congregation after them) — however, before you take it to the board, work through (in your mind) what might be some different ways that the budget could morph and change. You will want to have your own opinions on these matters *before* the meeting with the church board. (For instance, if they were to insist that the budget be cut by 5%, you would already know what line items you think should be cut.)

-Generally speaking, if the budget is about the same, or even lower, than the previous year it is often approved rather easily unless there is a serious issue consuming the church. If the budget is significantly higher than the previous year, you're likely going to have to start cutting - unless the church is busting at the seams and the dollars are rapidly increasing. If the proposed budget is somewhat higher than last year — everyone will be in for plenty of discussion.

-Be sure to look over your giving totals from the last couple of years at the church (and relate them to attendance figures) this will give you a reasonable sense of what is financially possible. Divide the total giving for a year by the number of average Sunday attendees. If you do this going back for a few years- you should gain a reasonable idea of how many people it takes to meet a certain budget number. This not an exact science but more like a common-sense approach.

-If you realize that the proposed budget is too high, you and the board may just start cutting the budget right there. Depending on what is being discussed, you may need to go back and meet with your staff and then come back to the board for approval.

-Doggedly guard budgets for *outreach*. This is an essential ministry of the church and it is the only path that could lead to a growing budget down the road. If the church wants to impact more people, and if various ministries want their budgets to grow, you will need more people at the church. Cutting monies for outreach is guaranteeing that the future is less than desirous.

Overseeing Budgets:

-It is crucial that the pastor is viewed as competent in this arena. Negligence can severely hamper your ministry.

-Basically, whoever oversees a line item spends as they see fit. This individual also approves the expenditures of those under them. (But when it's gone, it's gone.) It can be helpful to adopt a policy that if spending over a certain amount (say $500.00) all at once, that the finance person is given a heads up.

-All receipts need to be turned in monthly — complete with an attached form that describes the item purchased, what line item on the budget it corresponds to, and the purpose of the expenditure.

-Individual reimbursements should operate the same way.

-The finance team should generate a monthly report on spending totals for the year, compared to budget, for each item. As well as spending, expenditures, and giving on a month to month basis. (These should be reviewed by the church board). Occasionally, you will then need to go back to the board to readjust the budget: if giving is way down or if attendance at a ministry suddenly spikes. It may also be helpful to discuss these reports with your staff.

Financial Safeguards And Common Practices:

-Pay for an outside audit or book review annually. You *cannot* afford to mismanage money. It will doom your ministry. If people believe that anything is amiss with budgeting and accounting — your donations and ministry will like dry up.

-Make sure that two different signatures are needed on checks. And that at least two different people count offerings and record the totals.

-If giving is decreasing, share stories and cast vision on Sundays, make an announcement concerning the financial status, send letters home, start cutting (salaries and outreach should be some of the last things, but sometimes you have no other choice).

-Keep in mind that most of the time, finances reflect the health of the church. Not always, but often. If giving is decreasing and there is not a clear reason (like a major depression in the local economy) this is a sign to you that something in the church is off and needs attention.

-Be a little leery of unbudgeted donated items given by laypeople and designated gifts (handle with charity — but be wise in accepting these). This can be a subtle way of people trying to manipulate the budget and even possibly the overall mission of the church.

-Make sure that detailed copies of the budget are always public and available. This creates trust. Record weekly giving and the weekly budget, and year to date giving and budget, on the weekly bulletin. People feel confident in giving to ministries that are open and honest about the books.

-Make it very easy for people to give to the church: pass the plate, giving boxes in the back, online giving, texting, repeating bank withdrawals, and more.

Social Media
And Socially Responsible Marketing

A church cannot reach people who are unaware of their existence or what they may have to offer. Church marketing (that younger church leaders can live with) is explored.

"The marketer's job... is to tell a true story, one that resonates, one that matters to people, and to repeat it often enough that it creates value."

-Seth Godin

"Great marketing just makes a bad product fail faster."

-David Ogilvy

"How, then, can they call on the one they have not believed in? And how can they believe in the one of whom they have not heard? And how can they hear without someone preaching to them?"

-Romans 10:14

Why Marketing And Social Media:
-Unless you pastor a church with a 1,000 or more people- many people have no idea that your church even *exists*. Yes, even people who live relatively close to your church facility — likely have no idea that you are there. We tend to forget this — because we think about the church all the time. But just like that restaurant that you might drive by every day and have never thought twice about, this is how many people experience your church. (An important regular discipline for a working pastor is to attempt to *force* yourself to try to see your church ministry the way that most "outsiders" see it, which means often, not seeing it at all.)
-If you want to connect with people, and see them come to faith in Christ, marketing of some form, *must* be a priority. Many younger church leaders have been rightly turned off by slick, disingenuous, and unscrupulous marketing. Yet some have swung the pendulum the other

82

way, and because they refuse to get the word out about their church, their ministry suffers. The solution to shallow and manipulative marketing doesn't have to be the absence of all marketing. (Call it *networking* if it makes you feel better, but either way, it must be a priority if you truly want to engage in mission.)

-It is impossible to get the word out, appropriately, to everyone. We live in a fragmented culture, there is no longer such person as the "average American." Therefore, all marketing initiatives should be created and tailored for the right kind of people — the people who are "just outside of faith" — but that are spiritually open, and would likely connect with your specific church. (People who fit your target *mindset*.)

-The marketing channels that you might use- billboards, newspaper, radio ads, and social media likely depend on the region of the country your church is located within, and the psychographics of those whom your church is likely to connect with. What are the channels or specific forms of media, that the people you are targeting, tend to consume?

Possible Marketing Channels:

-The church's **website** does need to function as an online brochure for an outsider — but having a website does not itself, equal marketing.

-**Mailers**: typically, postcards that are mass-mailed to homes. The jury is out if these are still effective or not. They might work if: 1)You design the mailers to completely fit who you are (you don't buy them pre-made, they have more of a *boutique* vibe and not a *mass-produced* vibe.) 2) You use a marketing company to get a list of addresses that are chosen based on specific criteria. 3)They are sent repeatedly to the same people.

-**Signs at major intersections**: more effective than you may realize. (Especially if the signs are designed to stand out and the feel of your logo fits the culture of your church.) It's not unusual to see a few families visit your church each month simply from seeing the signs.

-**Regular social media posting**: These can work if they're consistent, interesting (most are not), and you regularly work at making more and more contacts.

-**Sponsored social media posts**: Fairly effective, again, if it they have interesting content. The type of content that would motivate a person to share it with someone else.

-**Pastors' blog**: only works if it is updated regularly, with very interesting content, and the pastor has real writing ability. (They key to being *interesting* includes writing content, with a style, that clearly draws in a specific kind of person but that also — turns *off* most other people.)

-**Video** always gets more eyeballs that print. Make videos more than print publications or audio files.

-**Old traditional media** (like an article in the newspaper or being covered by local television) is still way more effective than you might realize. It tends to get passed around. But you likely need someone in your church who understands public relations to aggressively pursue these channels. (It often takes work to get the media to cover you.) And you must be doing something truly interesting — something that *is* newsworthy.

-But in general, as important as marketing is, it will not work if your church is not worth remarking about. Your church needs to be interesting to a specific kind of person or none of this will work. But again, there are some interesting and honorable churches, whom are not connecting with people, simply because they lack proper marketing initiatives.

Philosophy:

-For someone to consciously recognize your church, they often need to hear about it in some form, *multiple* times. Usually, various marketing and social media efforts all work together, to rise within someone's consciousness. One channel alone is rarely effective.

-Of course, *word of mouth is the most effective form of marketing*. In reality, only about 3% of church goers have the desire and/or ability to enlist friends to check out a ministry with them. Word of mouth often works as the "sole" marketing strategy *only if* you are a very large church.

-The only way to gain traction in most marketing (especially social media) strategies is to offer an angle with a little "edge" to it — one that is slightly controversial. This does not mean being offensive. Generic, "for everybody" initiatives are boring and get lost. *If someone doesn't like it — it won't get the eyeballs of other people*. But, you should keep in mind that anything online, never goes away. This requires real strategic thinking ahead of time.

-Additionally, social media only tends to work if it is engaged repeatedly and you have something to offer beyond "come to our church." Part of the reason for engaging this marketing initiative — is hoping that people will eventually check out your church. But that angle alone is rather meaningless.

-Wise church leaders budget a decent amount of money for marketing and social media. If done well, this is money well spent. If it helps you to connect with people and to genuinely reach some of them — it more than pays for itself economically and even more for the sake of the kingdom.

Implementation:

-Remember there is a huge gulf between digital natives and digital immigrants. The specific channels you chose should be in alignment with whom you are hoping to connect with, and, with who you are as a church.

-Young people, obviously, understand how social media works. Use them to help you design your strategic initiatives.

-It is crucial that your marketing efforts honestly reflect who you *are* as a church. People who receive these messages and show up should feel that who you are as a church is *exactly what they expected*. This means absolutely zero false advertising. You cannot give the impression that your church is filled with young people if it is mainly made up of older people. You cannot claim to be multi-cultural and multi-ethnic if almost everyone is white. Never use stock photos, only legit ones.

-As the pastor, you will be held personally responsible for all marketing and social media that goes out from the church. Either oversee it yourself, or delegate it to someone more knowledgeable, but make sure that you give final approval before it goes out.

Loving People Through Staying Above The Law

Shepherding a congregation includes protecting them. An exploration of common legal vulnerabilities, and how to negate them, is crucial in a litigious society.

"The work of managing churches and church institutions races on, expanding into areas as diverse as procedures for legal incorporation of church-sponsored activities, prevention of sexual harassment and abuse, public relations, and legal liabilities in leasing church facilities to community organizations."

-T.E. Frank

"The primary vice in referring to the Bible... is that such an argument may diminish the jury's sense of responsibility for its verdict and imply that another, higher law should be applied... displacing the law in the court's instructions."

-People v. Huggins

"Whoever rebels against the authority is rebelling against what God has instituted, and those who do so will bring judgment on them-selves."

-Romans 13:2

Getting Started:
-Overseeing the church's legal obligations and risk factors *is* part of your job. This is part of why people *pay* you. It is *essential* that you educate yourself thoroughly enough on legal issues to adequately protect the church and your parishioners. People have invested dollars, talent, and years of their life into this ministry. They surely do not want to see it suffer through executive negligence. Overseeing and managing legal issues and risk certainly is not fun but to disregard this is to disregard the people of the church.
-Talk to and consult with your church insurance agent. (It is to their

advantage to make sure that you are adequately protected.) Make sure that the church has enough coverage. Quite often, denominations will provide insurance coverage guidelines. Additionally, your insurance company can provide you with plenty of advice on the best way for churches to develop procedures and policies for various events and which type of activities should be avoided at all costs. The insurance company is your friend — it is their business to know how the law and courts work.

Children And Youth Ministries:

-Parents or legal guardians must fill out a permission form for any events that are *away* from the church facility or in which parents are not present. A copy of these records, complete with emergency contact numbers and/or insurance information, must be taken with youth leaders on all trips.

-Many insurance companies will not cover any events involving: snow skiing, backyard swimming pools, or trampolines. Be sure to check with them before these activities.

-*All* adults working with children and youth (paid staff and volunteer) *must* receive formal training on appropriate and inappropriate relationships and interactions. Strict guidelines must be codified in writing and all who work with children and youth will need to sign that they will abide by them. This includes *driving* and *participation* guidelines.

-Some typical guidelines (but not an exhaustive list):
    -an adult is never to be alone with a child
    -no wedgees or touching of undergarments, or anything even similar to touching
    -no kissing, sitting on laps
    -at least one male leader and one female leader must be on all trips
    -children are NEVER to receive bathroom assistance — diapers are to be changed in full view of others
    -children and youth are NEVER to be physically disciplined or verbally shamed - light-hearted teasing must be handled very wisely

-Background checks should be completed on those who volunteer with teens and/or children.

-Children's ministry needs a thoroughly considered check in/out procedure. Part of this is to ensure proper safety (someone cannot walk off with a child) and part of this is due to heightened expectations of parents. Your safety procedures will not be judged alongside other churches but alongside professional daycare and preschool centers.

-All staff should be instructed to share the details about *every possible incident and concern* (no matter how small) with the senior pastor immediately. He/she should never be in the dark about any possible problems. Bad things happen when a parent contacts the senior pastor about an incident and the senior pastor is completely unaware of what happened. In the event of any type of incident or complaint — a detailed written record should be kept on file.

-*Watch out for*: an adult volunteer that has a "special" relationship with a particular teen or child. Be leery of recruiting the super fun (yet immature) adult to work with the teens.

Other Common Legal Issues:

-It is potentially *illegal* for you to share (even with other pastoral staff) what someone shares with you privately in your role as a pastor. You *can* be successfully sued for this. The same goes for talking publicly about infractions of a church member. In general, unless others are in danger or at risk, you should avoid discussing issues surrounding a church member's personal life with other people. The exception would be serious immoral infractions committed by a church staff member and/or issues of abuse.

-However, if you are notified that a staff member or volunteer is abusing a child you *must* report this to police. If you neglect to do this, you and the church can be legally liable, you will have lost all credibility with the public, and even contributed to the abuse of a precious individual.

-Have an attorney look over, and give you counsel, concerning hiring and firing procedures, church discipline matters, church by-laws, and all legal areas. Attorneys are not cheap, though many offer non-profit rates. However, money spent on legal counsel and guidance is usually well spent.

-According to the IRS, it is a legal infraction for a religious organization (that is tax-exempt) to explicitly engage in endorsing political candidates. What constitutes acceptable political activities is a bit of a grey area but it is something to keep in mind. Having the church lose its tax-exempt status, most likely, would mean shutting the doors permanently. It *has* happened before.

-If someone gives money to the church for a specific project or ministry (missions' trip, building fund, new organ, or whatever) it is *illegal* for the church to spend the money on anything else (including the general operating budget). It is not uncommon for churches to get into legal trouble for this type of infraction.

-Create a thought-through strategy to minimize the possibility of the misuse of funds:

> -who has credit cards, how they are used, (requiring receipts for all purchases along with explanation of purchase)
> -require two different signatures for all checks
> -three or more people count the week's offerings (and they all record the total)
> -hire an outside accounting agency to set up your financial procedures and to do an annual review of the financial books

-Remember, board members and staff can be held *legally* responsible if someone misuses funds, abuses a child, and more if reasonable procedures have not been created to prevent these issues. The privilege of leading a ministry comes with legal responsibility.

Handling Ministries

Helping Visitors Know That
They Are Welcomed

All churches want visitors; few make the most of following up with them after the first contact. This section offers a how to guide for effective assimilation.

"In the light of Jesus' life, death, resurrection, and return, Christian hospitality is the intentional, responsible, and caring act or welcoming or visiting, in either public or private places, those who are strangers, enemies, or distressed, without regard for reciprocation."

-Arthur Sutherland

"As a way of life, an act of love, an expression of faith, our hospitality reflects and anticipates God's welcome. Simultaneously costly and wonderfully rewarding, hospitality often involves small deaths and little resurrections. By God's grace we can grow more willing, more eager, to open the door."

-Christine Pohl

"Love each other deeply, because love covers over a multitude of sins. Offer hospitality to one another without grumbling."

-1 Peter 4:8-9

Before People Walk In The Door:
-It is easier to turn a first-time visitor into an engaged member of the church than it is to get someone to show up for the first time. Therefore, it behooves you to work hard at assimilating new people! Churches that are growing tend to retain more visitors than churches who are not.
-Remember, the church website is a brochure for potential first-time visitors. Invest in it, make sure it is of high quality (which does *not* mean complex) and create it with *outsiders* in mind. Clearly answer *their* questions on your site: Sunday times, what you do for children, how most people dress for worship, a rundown of a typical service, audio or video of sermons, biographies of the staff, clear directions to

your place of worship, genuine pictures and/or videos of your people and facility (as opposed to stock photos), etc. Elements like your governing structure, or a highly detailed statement of faith, do not need to be on your website. These are *insider* matters and rarely questions of first time guests.

-Have very clear signage outside of your building (and at main roads or intersections along the way) so that it is easy to find your facility.

-Depending on the size of your church, parking attendants may be useful.

When People Walk in the Door:

-Have adequately trained greeters who pleasantly welcome people and hand them a bulletin. New people like to be able to read about the latest happenings and it gives introverts something to do. (Do *not* assume everyone who visits is an extrovert.) If you are not handing people a bulletin, they are likely simply looking at their phone before worship begins.

-Enlist some of your out-going members to serve as wandering "friends" in the lobby who look for new people and introduce themselves, help them find coffee and refreshments (yes you must have these) and who can lead parents to the children's area. (Children's ministry needs clear signage from the lobby as well.) They should also hand visitors a quality welcome packet complete with a simple run down of various ministries (with contact information of key leaders), a clear description of the distinctives of the church (don't think theological statements here — think of the experience of new people), and most importantly, a contact card and pen.

-The contact card should ask visitors for their name, children's name and ages, phone number, address, email address, etc. They can indicate if they would like to speak to a pastor, if they have a prayer concern, etc.

-If people have children, they must *also* be warmly greeted by trained volunteers with a clear, professional check-in system and be handed some information on children's ministry. (People really want to know what will be happening with their children.)

-EVERY Sunday, share announcements as if for first time visitors: thank them for coming, clearly explain events without insider jargon, and mention the welcome packet and contact card. Let them know that they can either drop the contact card in the offering plate or hand it to the person who gives announcements in the lobby after worship.

Following Up with Visitors:

-After their first visit: a staff member should call them (though it almost always goes to voicemail), they should be sent an email from a key lay person or small group leader, and have a tasteful gift and letter delivered to their house on Monday. Additionally, friend request them on appropriate social media platforms.

-After their second visit: a staff person should snail mail them a personal note and their children should each individually receive a snail mail note from a children's ministry staff member.

-After their third visit, if your church is smaller or mid-sized, a staff member should meet them for coffee to get to know them briefly, encourage them to check out a small group, and to enlist them to volunteer. (People who attend small groups and who volunteer almost always stick around. People who won't do either are often gone in a few weeks- you might as well go for it.) If it is a larger church, they could be invited to a new visitor's monthly lunch immediately after worship. At the lunch, the senior pastor should share the story of the church, facilitate new people getting to know each other, answers any questions, and encourage them to join a small group and volunteer in some capacity.

-It makes very little sense to avoid enlisting third time visitors to volunteer, if they are offended or are highly reluctant, it is unlikely they will stick around anyway.

Membership Just Might Matter

Church membership largely appears to be on the way out. At the same time, if church leaders want to see their ministries thrive, they just might need to find a way that emphasizes personal commitment.

"There's nobody who doesn't have problems with the church, because there's sin in the church. But there's no other place to be a Christian except the church."

-Eugene H. Peterson

"By choosing... to stay... even in the teeth of my struggles with problems I perceived in the church, I was making it possible for the church to correct me and to give me a fuller picture."

-Jake Meador

"Let us consider how we may spur one another on toward love and good deeds, not giving up meeting together, as some are in the habit of doing, but encouraging one another."

-Hebrews 10:24-25

The Benefits Of Official Church Membership:
-Some younger church leaders (with a goal to create a church that feels approachable) may tend to down-play official church membership. This may be a mistake. If people never officially "belong" they tend to hang back in their commitment to the church and to Jesus. It is much easier for them to bail on the church when things get rocky. It could be just another manifestation of the late-modern consumeristic mindset. Even "community" becomes a commodity.
-Consider framing church membership like a wedding ceremony: you did not fall in love on your wedding day but genuine love will always make *public commitments*. Following Jesus is always personal, but it is never private.
-In some circles, membership (like baptism) becomes the "line-crossing" activity when making a profession of faith. (Like the sinners'

prayer.) This is especially true with more educated and professional people or people with a high-church background.

-Membership can also aid others in coming to faith in Jesus. When the entire church gains a reputation as being a community of love and service and authenticity, it is easier for people to buy into the reality of the lordship of Christ. If people simply think that one individual is a great person, others do not typically assign the credit to Christ himself.

-The missional genius of church membership is that it allows you to have "high-standards" for believers, while simultaneously posturing yourself as a highly welcoming community for all kinds of sinners. Since most people come to faith within a church community, you will want to create a church where all kinds of sinners can be highly involved. But to not lose a sense of *otherness* and *transcendence* (which is essential for life change) you will need to maintain rather high standards for official Christians. Membership can allow you to do this. Your official members become your "official" Christians (in which you maintain high standards for) and then with everyone else, you can simply accept them with everyone else, you are simply excited to have them around.

Evangelizing People For Membership:

-Like nearly every church activity, you will need to plan membership processes way ahead of time and over communicate them. When you feel like you are sick of saying something, people are finally beginning to hear it.

-Most of the time, you (or someone else) will need to recruit people into taking membership steps. People are allergic to commitment these days and so they often need some gentle encouragement to consider membership. Personal notes and phone calls to people who "appear ready" are very appropriate - as well as conversations in person. Be sure to include any new regular attendee on this list, even if they are quite new to the church. Many people who come to the initial membership class won't be ready for an official commitment yet. However, simply attending the class can help new people stick around and get attached to the church.

-Young singles are the most difficult group to lead to consider membership, but once you get a couple of them, sometimes, their friends will come along!

Leading A Membership Class (But Call It Something Else!):
-It's likely not possible to have official membership without some version of a membership class.

-Be sure you investigated any denominational procedures or protocols ahead of time, so that everything that you do and say will be within bounds!

-During an effective class:
> -People get to interact with the pastor(s) in a smaller/social environment.
> -People hear the story of the church and they share their personal stories with each other. (Even if they are not yet a believer!)
> -People learn the key theological beliefs of the church (but in a "heart-way," not merely as an informational dump).
> -People have plenty of time to ask any questions they may have.
> -People hear the vision and values of the church.
> -People interact seriously and personally with what it means to be a follower of Jesus.
> -People hear primarily from the senior pastor, but they also get to meet other key staff leaders.
> -People learn about all the various ministries of the church.
> -People receive a professional looking notebook that contains all necessary information in print so that they can take it home with them and review it as needed.

-It is probably most effective and enjoyable to host these at the pastor's home if possible or at least in another casual setting. Offer *good* food and drink so that people enjoy being there. Offer childcare as well. Pay someone if need be.

-*Part of your goal during these classes is for new people to get to know one another.* It is unlikely that new people will find community with long-term members of the church. They already have their friends. They will most likely find it with each other. You want to facilitate this as much as you can.

Making Membership A Big Freakin' Deal:
-You do not want membership standards to be too light, they will water down your church. Churches with high membership standards tend to be much more effective in ministry, regularly see lives change, and more effectively bring transformation to their neighborhoods. When you have higher standards, people stay more involved and engaged. The

more people who stay involved and engaged, the more enticing the church becomes, and the church has more energy to make a difference in others' lives. Churches with "low standards" really struggle.

-Remember, traditionally speaking, church membership and salvation went hand in hand. Biblically, there are no "solo" Christians. Many churches require baptism as part of membership.

-A few ways in which you can make the membership process "challenging": require a class that meets more than once, require candidates to meet with and have a "sponsor," require candidates to sign a membership covenant, maybe even consider facilitating the traditional love feast (communion, shared meal, and feet washing)?

-The membership covenant should include and acknowledge that they: trust in and follow Jesus as Lord, support the leadership of the church, support the official church doctrinal statements, will give financially, will serve regularly, will engage relationally with church members, and finally that they are open to church discipline (if need be) and that they recognize that membership can be revoked.

-Find a way to make it a big deal and recognize new members. A special gathering for them when they first join or have them stand and lay hands on them and pray for them during a Sunday morning, have them share their stories publicly, and so on. These public, symbolic recognitions are very transformative for people. Additionally, they tend to pump up the people in your church.

-You will likely want to send them an official letter (on church letterhead) recognizing their membership.

-You will need to send some official letters if members do not show up for some time. (Maybe two or three months?) The purpose of these official letters is to inquire if they are still members and remind them that they have committed to participation within the local church. But obviously to do this, you must keep up with people in some form.

Inviting Others Into Ministry

Younger pastors excel at friendliness, yet often struggling with equipping volunteers and giving ministry away. The case and strategies for enlisting volunteers are highlighted.

"Words and work are one… body and soul are one… the individual and the group are one."

-Jacob J. Enz

"There is a unique relational bond which comes from 'being in the foxhole' with someone and serving together. I have made literally hundreds of personal connections and lifelong friends because of volunteering."

-Brian Dodd

"We have different gifts, according to the grace given to each of us. If your gift is prophesying, then prophesy in accordance with your faith; if it is serving, then serve; if it is teaching, then teach; if it is to encourage, then give encouragement; if it is giving, then give generously; if it is to lead, do it diligently; if it is to show mercy, do it cheerfully.

-Romans 12:6-8

The Value Of Volunteering:
-Few (if any) people enjoy being involved with a church over the long term if they are *not* regularly volunteering. Serving provides people with a sense of ownership of the ministry and excites them about their faith. It may even provide many people with a sense of meaning. (This may sound silly to you, but I assure you, it does not to *them*.)

-People do not show up to watch you minister. People want to be *involved*. This gives them a sense that God is working within their life. Even if they have a great job, most people feel that it provides them a living, but not a sense of meaning.

-Some pastors fear that they are going to burn people out. This will not happen (even in key volunteer positions) *if* the position fits their strengths and their gifts. When people use their gifts, they too become energized. Burnout almost always arises when someone is regularly asked to do something that they do not enjoy doing or are not naturally gifted for.

-If people are burning out (and they are in a position using their gifts) it is often due to poor organizational structures more than volunteering. (Or, they are not adequately utilizing other volunteers in their ministry area and they are carrying the entire burden themselves.) Key volunteers (in leadership position) need to be encouraged, taught, and assisted with recruiting *other* volunteers.

-The "secret" job of a pastor *is to recruit other people to do the things, that people assume, that they get paid to do.* Likewise, the task of key volunteers *is to recruit other people to do the things, that people assume, they volunteered to do.*

Making The Ask:

-It is always best to ask people personally to volunteer in the church. You will get a much higher percentage of people who will agree to volunteer if you do so. This puts the onus on them to say *no* instead of saying *yes*. Some will turn you down, but the clear majority will not *if* you ask them personally.

-Mass appeals generally do not work, unless it is for a one-time special event. In that case, you will either want to have sign-up sheets in the lobby or even pass them through the rows on Sunday. Make it clear, that for this event, "everyone" is doing something.

-At least initially, you will get some more takers if people can volunteer for a definite period: six months, a year, than if it is for an indefinite period. (This way they do not feel trapped as if they were signing away their life forever.) Quite often, they will "re-up" their commitment after the initial season of volunteering.

What Volunteers Need:

-All volunteers want to clearly know what is expected of them and what it will look like for them to be successful. They will need a role description and some training with clear, step-by-step instructions. They don't want to have to think too much about this. They need answered: "What exactly am I being asked to do? When? How? Where? And of course: *Why?*"

-If they are volunteering in a leadership position they will need a role description, ongoing training and staff meetings, some one-on-one meetings, and lots of thanks. However, leaders should be given room to figure *how* to do what it is that you are asking of them on their own. The typical volunteer wants everything to be very clear and simple for them. The natural leader (who is taking on an influential role) often desires plenty of feedback, but also, more room to do what they do. People with strong leadership gifts will rarely stick in a church that wants to micro-manage their ministry.

-In general, the volunteers do the work of the ministry and the pastor's job is to recruit them, train them, thank them, cheer them — remind them of the larger purpose of *why* they do what they do (lots of meaningful stories), *and* to remove obstacles for them to make their ministry easier for them.

-All volunteers need to be provided with a schedule of when they are serving (months in advance), complete with contact info for all the other volunteers in their ministry. It should be *their* responsibility to contact another volunteer and switch volunteer dates with them if they cannot be there for some reason. You do not want this to fall on the staff. It will overwhelm people and little ministry will be accomplished.

-Volunteers are "paid" through finding meaning in their service, experiencing community through shared serving, and getting some time with the pastor. Highest volunteers should receive plenty of time from you. They should be treated differently than everybody else. The more responsibility they have, the more leeway they should be given, in how they implement their work. This may sound strange, but many people find getting close to a pastor as rather intriguing and somewhat insightful.

-Make volunteering (and their meetings) as cool and enjoyable as possible. It is also a good idea to have an annual thank-you event for volunteers- at minimum, for the volunteers in leadership positions.

A Culture Of Volunteerism:

-In general, within smaller and struggling churches, the lay people lead, and the staff do the ministry. In larger and thriving churches, the staff lead, and the lay people do the work of the ministry.

-Make it your goal to create a culture where *everyone* volunteers. This creates an alive "buzz" for your church and no one burns out. All the work is spread around, and people feel like "God is up to something." The experience of a very engaged church is rather engaging for anyone who engages it.

-This includes getting new people volunteering *as soon as possible*. Always have some designated spots (or even create some) that are simple and straightforward, where you can plug in new people. (Yes, make up jobs for them to do if needed.)

-Obviously this includes "non-Christians." There are always some spots where it would be inappropriate for a non-Christian to serve. But they are probably fewer than many imagine. Additionally, you may want to think through ahead of time (and put in writing) personal character expectations for leadership roles. This whole process will benefit from you having an organized system of getting to know people and their gifts. Then you can put them in a role that best fits them.

-Always keep a database of everyone who is serving and *where* they are serving. Talk as a staff team before you enlist someone into a new role and out of a previous one. Supply key leaders with a list of "leads" of newer people or regulars who are not currently serving from which they can recruit volunteers.

-There are always some staff people who are naturally gifted at recruiting people - use them!

-Be *slow* to pay people for service. Whenever humanly possible, enlist volunteers. The only time you should pay people is if: it requires hours and hours on a weekly basis like janitorial work, if you *must* have a professional in the position (accounting), or if it is a position that requires serious leadership skills and overseeing scores of volunteers. If you pay too many people, you kill a culture of volunteerism, and you will likely poison the church. This can be *deadly* to a ministry.

-Almost all of us, if we are honest, only have one or two strong gifts. If you hire someone, you are most likely paying them for that "one real skill" that they could likely accomplish in a relatively short amount of time as a volunteer. Paying them, many times, does not add more value to the church. You end up paying them for that "one real skill" and largely, to do many other things in which they are not gifted. A volunteer, using their God-given gift, can often accomplish more in two hours than a paid staff member, who lacks the gift, might in fifteen hours.

-Occasionally you may want to do something for someone who has had to go above and beyond for a season (overseeing a new building project, etc.) But even then, do not pay them, buy them a very special gift and take them out to a nice dinner as a thank-you.

Children, Youth, and Legal Considerations:

-In children's ministry, the more volunteers, the merrier everyone will be. Hit up all parents (Mom *and* Dad), some younger people, teens, older people who love kids, etc.

-For youth- look for *mature* adults, who are responsible, and who love teens. Be wary of the 40-year old, who acts like a 20-year old, when it comes to volunteering with teenagers. This can be a recipe for a disaster.

-All volunteers for children and youth ministries need to fill out a background check, read and sign a "do and do not" protocol list, and attend a clear behavioral and ethics training class. Check with your attorney and insurance company when preparing for these.

Creating Community Through Groups

Small groups and fellowship groups are common in contemporary ministry. But there are simple, yet often neglected, methods to make sure that they work for everybody.

"The man who articulates the movements of his inner life, who can give names to his varied experiences, need no longer be a victim of himself, but is able slowly and consistently to remove the obstacles that prevent the spirit from entering. He is able to create space for him who heart is greater than his, whose eyes see more than his, and whose hands can heal more than his."

-Henri Nouwen

"Be human in this most inhuman of ages; guard the image of man for it is the image of God."

-Thomas Merton

"Be devoted to one another in love. Honor one another above your-selves. Never be lacking in zeal, but keep your spiritual fervor, serving the Lord. Be joyful in hope, patient in affliction, faithful in prayer. Share with the Lord's people who are in need. Practice hospitality. Bless those who persecute you; bless and do not curse. Rejoice with those who rejoice; mourn with those who mourn. Live in harmony with one another."

-Romans 12:10-16

Purpose Of Small Groups:
-Small groups are nearly essential today. In the past, most people "automatically" joined churches. Participating in Sunday worship was enough for them. Besides, they lived in small knit communities and they naturally mingled with people from the church in their social lives on a consistent basis. But in today's world, relationships are more highly valued. Small groups easily create contexts for meaningful connection. Particularly as a church grows, organized forms of relationship-building

are needed. (Though in a church of under 75 people, they are rarely needed. That church *is* a small group.)

-Organized groups are essential because you cannot create community by "simply hanging out together." Community develops around organized *activities*. Most people will not feel like groups are worth their time if you do not provide some type of organized Bible-based discussion.

-The general purpose of small groups is to facilitate relational connections with God and other people.

Small Groups' Leaders:

-Groups work best when their leaders are considered the "pastor" of the group. They are the first line of spiritual care and oversight for many people. They organize meals for people in a bind, visit them in the hospital, and the like.

-Groups need the trust of the senior pastor for them to work. The pastor is quite literally handing off much of the personal sharing, personal spirituality, and personal caring for church members to this small group leader. This is essential, yet it can also test how much a pastor trusts that the Spirit works through others.

-However, group leaders need to see themselves as facilitators of discussion and care and *not* as *teachers*. Groups work when people can be honest and share openly. They lose much of their relational component when someone begins to "teach" during the small group time.

-Leaders should always have an *apprentice leader* who is learning to lead a group. This creates a ready supply of future leaders as new small groups are formed.

-Anyone (or any couple) who is a genuine follower of Jesus could serve as a leader, but groups tend to thrive if they are led by "people-people" who naturally tend to connect with and gather other people. A solid group leader is rather good at recruiting people to their group.

-Leaders should understand that not everyone in their group are necessarily Christians or are currently living a biblically inspired lifestyle. Their goal is not to correct these people — but to welcome them and allow them to share openly and honestly. If an unbeliever is in a small group and is accepted and cared for, they will tend to "just naturally" come to faith in Jesus over time, if people accept them and are not regularly trying to correct them.

-Small group leaders should be expected to attend quarterly training meetings and meet with a member of the staff regularly. Leaders tend to atrophy over time and they do require regular mentoring and training.

When And Where Groups Meet:

-Groups are often most meaningful when they meet in people's homes. They feel more intimate than in a church facility. This is also a way to get other people involved: some people lead, others host.

-In some highly religious areas, groups can meet weekly. But in most of the country, about every other week works best. In working class communities, mid-week gatherings can work. In more professional communities, Sunday evenings may be the only option.

-You must include clear "breaks" from groups. (If they simply meet indefinitely, people will be reluctant to lead or host. Also, they tend to lose momentum.) Take the month of December off. It may also be a good idea to break for the summer. These breaks allow people to join another group and for you to begin a new group. Groups that stay together too long become in-grown, gossipy, and unhealthy.

-There are various ways to begin new groups: simply starting a new one from scratch and purposefully inviting people who are new to the church to attend. Splitting a group in two (this should be done carefully). Or, having the leaders of a group begin a brand new one and their former apprentices take the helm of their old group.

General Schedule Of Small Groups Gatherings:

-Welcome people, hang out together, and enjoy refreshments — allow about thirty minutes

-Ice-breaker discussion: What was your most embarrassing moment from your teen years? What was the greatest Christmas gift you ever received? Interact around opening questions, like this one — ten minutes

-Guide based discussion involving scripture but primarily focused on sharing about their lives together — forty minutes

-Sharing of prayer requests and praying for each other — ten minutes

Small Group Guides:

-Some churches use official curriculum, others write their own thematic studies, and others create discussion guides based on the Sunday sermon.

-Regardless, you want guides that ask open-ended questions about people's lives mashed up with the Bible and not simply traditional

Bible study guides. You want to provoke honest, personal, sharing and discussion.

-Be sure to print guides. People looking at their phones kills community.

Miscellaneous:

-Try to get people in a small group as soon as possible. People in groups tend to stick in churches, people who do not get in one, rarely do.

-If you want anyone with children to be in a group — you must organize childcare for the group.

Some churches can get volunteers to do this — many simply hire babysitters.

-Some churches have gender specific small groups and others have blended ones. Gender specific groups often lead to people sharing in more detail about their lives. However, they lack learning from both sexes, and they can be harder to maintain. If spouses both belong to gender specific groups, this means there are two evenings when the whole family isn't together. This make take a toll over time.

Community Group Leadership Do's And Don'ts

DO

- Keep up personally with members as much as possible

- Ask them about their lives and pray with them

- Ask people to get involved and take on tasks such as bringing snacks, or contacting a new person, or caring for others

- Involve people as much as possible, ask them to share and participate

- Love, care, and encourage your members as much as you can

- Let Pastor _____ know what is happening in your group

- Work with your co-leader on who is doing what and keep in contact with one another

- Pray for your group members — God has given them to you to love

- Share your life with them and offer advice when solicited and appropriate

- Build bridges with people who are different than you and encourage the other group members to do the same

- Be sensitive that not everyone in your group has grown up in the church and is familiar with the Bible — expect this and be sensitive

- Let Pastor _____ know if there are serious issues with someone that is a part of your group

- Create an atmosphere where "what is said here, stays here"

- Help group members understand that they are safe to share personally in the group

DON'T
- Offer advice that is beyond you (such as suggesting they divorce someone, who they should marry, what meds they should or should not take)

- Lecture — these groups are for sharing and discussing, not for you to teach your personal views on everything. Remember, you are facilitating a group, not imparting your thoughts to everyone on every topic.

- Play favorites. We all have certain people we connect with and others that we don't. You are called to shepherd and love everyone in your group not only the ones you have a lot in common with or agree the most with.

- Demand that everyone agree with you. Please share your thoughts and offer insight. However, you don't help people by telling them they must see it your way or imply that they don't care about God. Keep in mind that this does not help develop or form people.

- Let any one person dominate the group (including yourself). There is always one person who wants to talk constantly and no one else can get a word in. Find creative ways of bringing out others' participation and if needed, ask if someone else can have a chance to share. Be wary of the "crisis of the day" person who wants to dominate each gathering with their recent crisis. You must do what is best for the whole group and not let one-person derail everything.

- Make this your personal bully pulpit for your politics or social stances. They may be shared kindly, but we are creating contexts where people are free to have different opinions and not feel shamed for disagreeing.

- Talk about what people shared in the group with others outside of the group, other than pastoral staff when necessary.

- Force people or pry into their personal lives if they do not feel comfortable sharing.

Throwing Parties For Sinners

Jesus (relationally and symbolically) hung out with sinners and helped them find redemption. Readers are encouraged to facilitate outreach gatherings that normal people want to attend.

"The relational and experiential nature of Christianity (relationship with God and others) means that it is available to all... It is not dependent on our comprehension... Experience may be provided for those who cannot comprehend."

-Arthur Freeman

"Conversion to... religious groups occurs when, other things being equal, people have or develop stronger attachments to members of the group than they have to nonmembers."

-Rodney Stark

"While Jesus was having dinner at Levi's house, many tax collectors and sinners were eating with him and his disciples, for there were many who followed him. When the teachers of the law who were Pharisees saw him eating with the sinners and tax collectors, they asked his disciples: 'Why does he eat with tax collectors and sinners?'"

-Mark 2:15-16

Reason And Purpose:
-There is *serious* value in leading your church to facilitate some *purposeful outreach events*. These help to keep outreach constantly in front of your people (if you, as the lead pastor, don't make outreach a priority, no one else will) and they provide people with a real reason to invite friends to your church. Healthy churches make outreach a priority. Churches that do not emphasize outreach are *almost always* unhealthy. These events tend to bolster the morale of the entire church.
-We are defining outreach events *as special gatherings that relationally connect with people outside of your church*. Social justice is important but that is a different kind of ministry.

Possible Outreach Events:

-In general, it is crucial that you plan out events that people outside of your church *would like to attend*. What *you* like and what *they* do are often not the same thing! Here is where the gulf between "church people" and "normal people" becomes rather apparent.

-Events for young families almost always work: carnivals, kids' movie nights, and more. Young families are always looking for things to do with their kids *and* they tend to be the most open to God compared to other life stages.

-VBS can really work *if* they are a "non-VBS" in tone. i.e. kids' weeks that involve genuine learning and Bible stories, teaching about other cultures and Bible stories, etc.

-If the church is big enough: sports' leagues and camps for children can be effective.

-Practical issues seminars: parenting, relationships, finances, and so on.

-In general, do not make these events overtly spiritual unless they are on a Sunday morning. You are attempting to build bridges with secular people and you want them to realize that you are more like them, and possibly have more to offer them, than they originally imagined.

-Special Sundays that acknowledge and celebrate certain groups: such as teachers, first responders, non-profit and social workers. However, you must sure to make special invitations to be sure that certain leaders representing these groups will be present and get input from others who represent these groups during your planning phase.

-Be sure to work the main religious holidays: Christmas Eve and Easter effectively. Make these events meaningful, spiritual, and yet *very focused* on outsiders. Find ways to make these special. Do not waste these opportunities.

-Even "bring a friend" Sundays can work within certain communities. This is where you pray, and plan, and communicate, and encourage everyone in the church to bring a friend on a certain day. Just be sure you do not call them "bring a friend day" during that morning!

Preparing For Outreach Events:

-You probably do not want to do any more than three or four of these a year. Any more than that and they lose their appeal and effectiveness. You can only call the whole church to action so many times before it loses its effectiveness.

-These events should be included in the church budget. The wise pastor pushes to make sure that outreach is always budgeted. This signals leadership vision. Besides, what kind of future will the church have if it is not investing in connecting with potential new members?

-Check school calendars *before* you plan the date of the event. Competing with the big high school football game, prom, and three-day weekends are a bad idea.

-In general, stay away from Saturday evenings if possible. People won't come back on Sunday. Friday nights, some Saturday afternoons, and Sundays after church, often work best.

-It may be helpful to hold these special events in the same location as where you worship. This helps people to associate this location and space with your church.

- Design everything for people who are somewhat spiritually open but are ignorant of the faith and are outside of the church. Obviously "chasing" people who are antagonistic to faith is a waste of time.

-Push hard for everything to be pulled off with *real quality*. It is better to do less and do it well — than to spread yourselves too thin. Quality communicates to people that you are competent and serious about your ministry. This means beginning to plan a minimum of four to five months ahead of time. Some events require a full year of planning and preparation.

-Depending on the type of event, see if you can get local businesses to donate items or at least to sell them to you at a reduced price.

-Be sure that everyone who attends is handed some quality (outsider focused) information about your church: when you meet, what Sundays are like, what you have for kids, and info on other future public events. If possible, collect their information as well and follow up with emails and snail mail that is designed for outsiders, as well as other types of appropriate personal follow-ups. Outreach events can be a waste of effort without disseminating info about the church and collecting their contact information.

Enlisting Leaders And Volunteers:
-Outreach events tend to get lay-people excited. Whenever possible, put them in charge of the event instead of staff.

-Put people who are gifted organizers and managers in charge, — not simply the people who are the most passionate about outreach. Personally seek out and enlist the most key people to to lead the team.

Attend the first planning meeting with them to share vision, see what questions people have, and to steer them in the right direction. But after this, only meet with the key person to assist them with any questions that come up and to coach them along in the planning process.

-Be sure that there are key people in charge of various aspects: promotion, parking, food, platform or entertainment, greeting, check-in. Be sure that they are prepared to train the volunteers underneath them in each area. Volunteers want their roles to be clear, simple, and time bound.

-Have sign-up sheets available on Sunday mornings for people to volunteer.

-Have some volunteers ready whose only job is to mingle and talk with guests and people who are sitting or hanging out by themselves.

-At the event, and on the Sunday afterward, make a big deal of everything that key volunteers did. Brag on the church and give the highlights on the following Sunday. Just be sure to do it in such a way that recognizes new people will be present at worship with you!

Promotion:
-Push outreach events hard in your church. In general, you need to feel like you are sick of talking about it for most people to really know what it is happening. Snail mail something to every home two months out and again two weeks out. Weekly emails and social media messages beginning six weeks out. Talk about it from the platform, preferably led by the senior pastor, every Sunday beginning six weeks out. This means telling stories of why people on the outside could truly benefit by connecting with your church. Hand everyone in your church postcards/ invitations designed to hand to their friends — a few weeks out. This includes children. Maybe even interview some "regular" people who are inviting others to share *why* they are inviting them. Have your small groups' leaders push these events as well.

-Do everything you can to get some local press coverage: this often means contacting them a few months out and contacting them *repeatedly*. Its good if a reporter shows up for the event. It's even better if they will interview you and do a story *before* the event. At minimum, give them a press release to include in their publications.

-*Note*: As important as these events are, they will ultimately be ineffective if your typical Sunday gatherings turn off outsiders and new people!

Embodying Love For The Neighborhood

Today, few people will join a church that is not making a practical difference locally. However, organizing people for neighborhood engagement is a whole other matter that needs attention.

[We should ask believers] "whether they find it normal that the churches should be religious clubs, so to speak, where people get together to comfort themselves with fine traditions while they forget all that is happening in the world."

-Sergio Rostagno

"Justice is the way that we can discover God."

-Dorothee Sölle

"He has shown you, O mortal, what is good. And what does the Lord require of you? To act justly and to love mercy and to walk humbly with your God."

-Micah 6:8

Purpose And Value:
-To be a healthy church, you likely will need to facilitate Sunday worship (public gathering), small groups (relationship building), deep discipleship (ongoing growth for committed believers), outreach events (evangelism), and social justice projects (tangibly blessing the neighborhoods). Many churches offer the first three of these. Healthy churches have all five. As within our personal lives, if there is an area where you are not "healthy" — it holds back the maturation of the whole. Ministry requires giving attention to the integrated whole of the church and not simply focusing where the pastor personally feels most comfortable or gifted. Your church must be more multi-faceted than *you* are as the pastor.
-Neighborhood projects have two purposes: 1) To practically and physically love your neighbors and 2) To provide a context where comfortable church people can find and partner with the Spirit in a new

and powerful manner. *Please do not dismiss this second purpose.* It is true that "poverty tourism" can be a problem. But historically speaking, followers of Jesus have always known that it was essential, for their own spiritual formation, to serve the poor. The Spirit does specific things within *committed believers* when they take this on as an embodied practice.

-Much of the ministry of Jesus involved *symbolic* actions. Jesus didn't overthrow the temple, but his "cleansing of the temple", and his inclusion of gentiles, symbolized the kingdom of God eventually expanding beyond national Judaism. Jesus did not overthrow the institution of slavery but his inclusion of outcasts symbolized the value of *all* people. Eventually, people began to see the evil of slavery. Likewise, part of the value of the church engaging in community service isn't always the change the church brings about, (this is much, much more difficult than many realize), but *the change that happens within some people within your ministry.* Of course, we would all like to be a part of real cultural change but this is often out of our hands. However, participating in the vision of Jesus can bring about real change. People will catch a vision and gain new values that will guide them as they make decisions in positions of power that they may occupy. For example, if you can help to facilitate wealthier, suburban professionals serving the poor, this may bring about a transformation within *them* that echoes well beyond your church's specific ministry.

What You Should Do As A Pastor:
-Part of your job (always) is to be plugged-in locally. The more the pastor is out of their office, in general, the healthier the church is — assuming this does not mean you are sitting at home watching Netflix. You need to have your ear to the ground to know what is happening in the neighborhood. You *are* the public face of the ministry. This includes "shaking hands and kissing babies" of local people and other local non-profits and ministries.

-If the people are primed for community engagement already — simply turn them loose and cheer them on!

-If the church has never really engaged their neighborhood, your job will be to *slowly* shift a culture so that people will begin to desire this on their own. Strong and immediate prophetic appeals often only result in your termination. The kingdom of Jesus needs pastors and prophets- but they are not often the same role.

1. Begin having initial conversations with your board and staff about

116

the importance of engaging the hurting people of your neighborhood.

2. Provide your board and staff with articles and books to read that tell stories of what other churches (who are like yours) have been doing. If the stories are of "idealized" churches that are radically different from yours — they will be dismissed as unrealistic and fanciful to your own congregation. These stories will start sparking imagination.

3. Begin preaching on Jesus and the early church's care for the "least of these."

4. Find some individuals in your church who already volunteer within local organizations and have them tell their stories on Sunday mornings.

5. When you have a sizable group that wonders why the church isn't doing something — (*this could take a few years*) plan a special day (after worship) for anyone who is interested to come to a meeting. Here, give them a *vision* and a few *guidelines*. Whatever they choose to take on, you want it to be *relational,* building relationships with other local people outside of the church's four walls. Additionally, encourage them to be bold — to do something that makes a real statement. There is symbolic value in these actions. Then leave them to decide as a group, how they believe the Spirit is leading them to serve and make a difference in the neighborhood.

6. Once they begin: give them a budget, coach them, and champion them, and have them share stories regularly about what God is doing on Sunday mornings. These don't have to be "big" stories, simply engaging stories. Find every meaningful way (video, object lessons, and more) to make a big deal about these initiatives and relationships during public worship.

-Remember, like everything, this project will only be sustainable if it becomes the work of the people of the congregation and not simply *your* work as the pastor.

-In general, unless it is a large church, it is best to stick with one project, year after year, building ongoing relationships and partnerships and making a serious difference over time. Over the long haul, this may change and expand. Clearly, the amount of local needs.

-One challenge here is that the amount of local needs are legion. To have any kind of helpful impact requires focus. This means there are many worthy and needed initiatives that you simply cannot take on.

-Once *this group* has been serving for some time, the *entire culture* of your church will begin to change. This does not mean that every single individual in your church will necessarily become personally involved-but as a whole, the values of your church will have been transformed.

The Delicate Dance To Walk:

-Social justice is championed in some communities, but not in all. This does not mean you shouldn't head down this path, but that you should — *carefully*. Most of America does not personally share the same concerns that young church leaders do! Churches and denominations that become *primarily known* for justice issues are often derided as "political" organizations. Recognizing this, have a thought through plan to assure that this label does not easily get attached to your congregation. As you move in this direction, think of how you will assure that you still give attention to personal spirituality, biblical instruction, communal relationships within the church, evangelism, and so on.

-This requires wisdom and subtleties on your part. If you do not lead the church towards justice issues the Spirit leaves the church. If you push too hard on these projects, you will be labeled as a liberal and you will lose many people from the church. Then where will your social justice projects be? This is a delicate dance to walk.

-Do your best to guide the church without people knowing where you are *politically*. No one should know what your personal politics are. Don't let yourself get pinned into any kind of ideological corner. Why would you want to blow up bridges to half of your church?

-Watch your preaching. Preaching works best when it is personal to the hearts of people. Guilting people about social causes tends to kill churches and leads some to too easily dismiss the preacher. Yet at the same time, highlight through illustrations and stories, what the Spirit is up to through the people of your church as they are engaging the neighborhood. You can move people along in the cause of justice, however, not as quickly as you would prefer.

-Prophets boldly name injustices and the reign of God - come what may. Religious administrators are mere keepers and overseers of what has always been. Pastors are involved in the long, careful work of moving people along to new places with God.

Spiritual Formation That Spiritually Forms

Young pastors know that calling people to "believe" is usually insufficient for making disciples. A model for life-changing discipleship (based on John Wesley's class meetings) is explored.

"There is within us a fundamental dis-ease, an unquenchable fire that renders us incapable, in this life, of ever coming to full peace. This desire lies at the center of our lives, in the marrow of our bones, and in the deep recesses of the soul. At the heart of all great literature, poetry, art, philosophy, psychology, and religion lies the naming and analyzing of this desire. Spirituality is, ultimately, about what we do with that desire."

-Ronald Rolheiser

"All spiritual disciplines have one purpose: to get rid of illusions so we can be present."

-Richard Rohr

"Make every effort to add to your faith goodness; and to goodness, knowledge; and to knowledge, self-control; and to self-control, perseverance; and to perseverance, godliness; and to godliness, mutual affection; and to mutual affection, love. For if you possess these qualities in increasing measure, they will keep you from being ineffective and unproductive in your knowledge of our Lord Jesus Christ."

-2 Peter 1:5-8

The Value And Purpose Of Spiritual Formation Groups:
-Your goal is to create an outlet for people who were committed to Jesus and who want to continue *further* in their discipleship. You want to create a path for people who after they come to faith, or had their faith rekindled after years of disillusionment, can *continue in discipleship* to Jesus and not feel they needed to "move on" to another church that has more to offer.

-However, you want this to be spiritually *motive-based* and not simply more information. The basic idea is to immerse people in practices, that over time, will bring about transformation and expose them to a method for continuing their path with Jesus.

-Specifically, you want people to engage a *process*. It's like coaching a kids' basketball team. There is not a specific practice or game where they "catch" it. But over an entire season off drills, scrimmages, coaching, and games their intuitive understanding of basketball will grow significantly. They will be playing at a much higher level.

Practically, set this up on two rails:

1. Communal discussions and spiritual practices *and*
2. Personal assignments to be done in-between bi-weekly gatherings.

You are hoping to hear, comments like the following, if your goals are being met:

"I am realizing that what Jesus is about is very different from what I care about."

"I realize I have been an admirer of Jesus and not a follower."

"God is awakening me to issues deep within that I did not know were there, and the things that He is doing- that I been completely ignorant of."

"It has become clear to me that people are incredibly lonely and most people have almost no one to really talk to."

Ground Rules:

-Do not give too much information ahead of time regarding what you will be doing. People may not think it sounds sexy enough. Simply announce that you are forming a group of people who want to go deeper spiritually, and that it will require real commitment. People must be willing to commit to every other Wednesday from January to May (for example) or they should not sign-up. Let people know that you certainly don't want anyone to join because they tend to just "show up" to all church activities.

-Require participants to keep a journal for the entire process. They are to bring the journal to meetings and write down in it as needed. They are to reflect in their journal on all personal assignments, etc. Your goal is that when they are finished with the spiritual formation group, they can look back through the journal and see all that God said, did, and changed within them. This will likely not happen quite as clearly without a written record of God's movement within their lives.

A Typical Meeting:
-Be a belligerent time keeper on these things. Each activity will go on forever if you allow them to. Keep time and work hard to keep everyone moving on schedule. If activities go over time, they tend lose their "punch."

7:00 - 7:10 - People arrive and small talk

7:10 - 7:30 - *Debrief* as an entire group on what they experienced and are discerning from their previous *assignments*. Do not allow people to respond, *"I learned that the Bible says..."* Only with what is happening *within their life* and what God is doing *within them*.

7:30 - 7:50 - Provide a *brief article, specifically on some topic of spiritual formation*. Read it together and spend some time discussing it. This is the only activity that is "informational." Your basic goal here is to provide them with different angles of understanding their life with God and what it means to be conformed to the image of Christ. Particularly, spiritual angles as opposed to "informational" approaches to discipleship.

7:50 - 8:10 Break in groups of two to three (gender specific groups) to *respond to the "Soul Questions."* For the sake of time and spontaneity, each person randomly picks two of the six questions to respond to each week. The purpose of these questions is to repeatedly lead them to consider various aspects of their life that they often give little thought to and to engage in talking honestly about their life with God. The Soul Questions are loosely based on John Wesley's questions for his class meetings.

Potential Soul Questions:
In what ways did God make his presence known to you since our last meeting?

In what ways did you encounter Christ in your reading of scripture and experiences of prayer since our last meeting? How has the Bible shaped the way you think and live?

How have you invested your money and spare time since we last met?

Is there anyone whom you fear, dislike, disown, criticize, hold resentment toward or disregard? Someone you are envious of? If so, what are you going to do about it?

What temptations did you face since our last meeting? How did you respond? Have you held something back from God that you need to surrender?

How did God provide an opportunity for you to share your faith with someone? How did you respond? What opportunities did the Spirit give you to serve and love others whom do not believe? How did you respond?

Who is in need that you are currently helping? How are you actively blessing someone who is in a bad place?

8:10 - 8:40 - Meditating And Hearing From Scripture
-At this point, gather back as an entire group, and guide participants through various types of spiritually listening to scripture. Maybe work from the Sermon on the Mount, and so each meeting, take ten to fifteen verses and use them for this time of meditation. Your goal here is for people to hear from God, but specifically, to expose them to different methods of personally engaging scripture beyond informationally based approaches. Guide them through what to do, step-by-step, through the process. (Don't explain the entire method but guide them long in an experience. "Now I want you to…" And then, "Okay, now…", and so on.) Afterward, debrief for a few minutes.

Examples Of Scripture Meditation Exercises:

Lectio Divina:
1. They pray silently for a minute or two.
2. They read the passage twice in a row out loud.
3. They quietly pray and ask God to bring a verse or phrase to mind.
4. They write down the verse or phrase.
5. They read the passage twice in a row out loud again.
6. They quietly pray and ask God what He is saying to them about that verse or phrase they wrote down.
7. They write down what they heard in prayer.
8. They read the passage twice in a row out loud for a final time.
9. They quietly pray and ask God what He wants them to do or become because of that verse or phrase He brought to mind.
10. They write what their heard in prayer down.

Humbling Approaching The Text:
1. They read the passage silently on their own.
2. Ask them to write down what phrase or verse for some reason "grabbed" them.
3. They read the passage again silently on their own.
4. Ask them to write down, what in this passage surprised them, how God said something or did something they would not expect.
5. They read the passage again silently on their own.
6. Ask them to write down what about the passage they simply do not understand at all.
7. Discuss together how the message of God is not something we can fully understand or always be confident that we know what God is up to.

Prayerful Imagining:
1. Read the passage.
2. Close your eyes and imagine you were physically there when Jesus originally spoke these words. What do you see? Write it down.
3. Read the passage.
4. Imagining you were there, again, what would you smell? Write it down.
5. Read the passage.
6. Imagining you were there with Jesus, what would physically touch or feel? Write it down.
7. Read the passage.
8. Imagining you were there, what would you hear? Write it down.
9. Read the passage.
10. Imaging you were there, what would you emotionally feel? Write it down.

8:40 - 8:55- Prayer
-Vary it each week, but either break-up in small groups or pray as a whole group together. The only kinds of prayer that should be permitted are the ones that center on what people are sensing from God, shortcomings they noticed within their lives, asking God to help them grow, etc. No one should be permitted to make requests for things or to pray for other people. (Such as, "My aunt is in the hospital...")

8:55 - 9:05- Giving Assignments

-Finish off the night by giving them assignments to do on their own for the next gathering. Remind them that these will not create "lightning bolt insights," but if they continue with the process, over several months they will become different people.

Offer 3 Kinds Of Assignments:

1. *Scripture Based*. The goal here is for people to personally soak in scripture (the same passages) for several months, so that when they are finished, they would have their imagination reformed. Perhaps your five months together could be based on the Sermon on the Mount (Matthew 5-7).

Assignments include:

Meeting one: read the sermon on the mount in one sitting, five times

Meeting two: read the sermon on the mount in one sitting, two times. Personally meditate (at other times) on Matthew 5:1-18, three different times.

Meeting three: read the sermon on the mount in one sitting, two times. Personally meditate (at other times) on Matthew 5:17-26, three different times.

2. *Personal-awareness Based*. The goal here is for people to discern (over the long haul) what God wants to do in their personal lives and to gain insight to the actual state of their hearts. This is purposefully a drawn-out process in order to create real understanding.

Assignments might include:

Meeting one: ask five or six friends to respond to the following questions about you personally, via email: 1) What words would you use to describe me? 2) What would you say are the strengths or gifts I bring to others? 3) What do you see as my weaknesses, or what do you wish was different about me? The questioner should not be encouraged to respond or to explain why they are this way.

Meeting two: summarize all the feedback you received from these friends and combine them into a couple of sentences, particularly about what people see as your faults.

Meeting three: provide two different friends with the summary of the feedback you received from the first group and ask them to explain why they think people said this about you. Again, the one asking the questions is not allowed to respond or explain. Only ask questions to understand what others are saying. The goal here is a deep understanding of the heart issues that they may have been blind to.

Here, we were hoping to build deep awareness about the patterns of sin in our lives. Eventually, you may craft "spiritual action plans" to hopefully grow in these areas. Maybe someone who comes to realize they are greedy may begin to meditate on certain bible passages on money, personally experiment with giving away items or cash to others, begin to log what they are thankful for that money can't buy, spend time with someone who is poor, or something similar.

3. **Others-focused Based**. The goal here is for people to become more like Christ by growing in their love and care of others who are outside of faith. Yes, we want people to come to saving faith. But your main goal is to use the vehicle of loving outsiders to spiritually form the participants.

Assignments Could Include:

Week One: Begin praying for someone you know who is not a follower of Jesus. It doesn't matter what you pray for about them — just pray for them.

Week Two: Get together socially with this person you have been praying for — have lunch, coffee, a beer, or whatever. Specifically listen to them. Do not share your faith. Do not talk much. Simply listen and try to understand them.

Week three: Begin praying for God's guidance in how you can meet a need for the friend that you have been listening to. What did they share with you as a need in their life? How might you meet it?

Eventually, you might also assign them to go out in the community at large and notice what needs exist that are not currently being met. This could culminate with the whole group "experimenting" (without you) on meeting a need in the community together. This could create a virus within the church that is marked by a desire to creatively reach out to others.

Loving Those Who Want To Learn

People tend to stay committed to organizations that teach them new things. Here, a vision for facilitating effective and practical classes and seminars is described.

"Jesus is not just nice, he is brilliant. He is the smartest man who ever lived."

-Dallas Willard

"The scandal of the evangelical mind is that there is not much of an evangelical mind."

-Mark A. Noll

"Love the Lord your God with all your heart and with all your soul and with all your strength and with all your mind."

-Luke 10:27

Purpose:
-Offering various classes or special seminars can help long-term, committed believers keep growing in their discipleship to Jesus. Or at least, they will *feel* like they help them to keep growing in their discipleship to Jesus! Long-term Christians seem to have a hankering to always "learn" more and to associate this with spiritual growth — which is not necessarily the case. You will need to offer some outlets in your ministry for people who already feel like they have "heard it all" and have "done it all." If you don't, people will feel like they need to move on to another ministry where they can keep learning and growing. You may disagree with their thinking about this, and possibly for good reason, but that does not change their personal desires. You cannot wish it away. If you want committed people in your ministry (people who volunteer and give money) you *must* give them a little bit of what they are looking for.
-Additionally, psychological research reveals that people tend to stay loyal to organizations of any kind if they believe that the organization

regularly *teaches them new things*. You may believe that some should have graduated from always needing to be "fed" and you may be right, but there are always people who feel like they need to learn more.

-On top of this, offering the right kind of seminars and classes can even serve as a tool for *outreach*. There are very few places, (within our culture, where people can gather to learn more about how to practically address common aspects of the human condition. If a church can offer some helpful seminars or classes — it might just be able to build some bridges to new people.

-There are basically two major types of classes or seminars churches offer: Bible-based learning and practical/topical based learning. Bible-based learning may include seminars like *"Investigating the Life And Times of the Revolutionary Jesus"* or *"Investigating the Origin and Nature of the Bible."* Practical-topical based learning could include *"How to Love a Person Who Doesn't Want to Change,"* *"Following Jesus with Your Wallet,"* or *"Parenting Teenagers in a Smart-Phone World."*

Preparing Classes And Seminars:

-Like everything in ministry, prepare these, at least to some degree, with "outsiders" in mind. The nature of these offerings does mean that they should be "meaty." But if you thread the needle correctly, you will also be able to make these *outreach events*. Not only in the practical topics (which are no brainers — take full advantage of these opportunities) but even in the Bible-based topics *if* you choose the right approach and give them an *appropriate* title.

-If you want these to be well attended, you will likely need to plan these months ahead of time. Find out the best nights of the week and the best times of the year: Sunday evenings? Wednesday evenings? Sunday through Tuesday during one specific week? For many churches, October-November, and February-April, work the best.

-It's often a good practice to bring in an outside expert for these seminars. People likely get tired of hearing from you, unless you are *particularly gifted* as a teacher, which isn't the same thing as being a *preacher*. If you are concerned that the outside expert may not naturally connect with your local congregation, you can have them share briefly, and then plan on interviewing them, and/or moderating other people asking questions. You are likely aware of the issues and questions of the people within your congregation. You can also serve as the "translator" if you feel like the content is not making sense to those in attendance. It probably is a good practice to have a time in every class where people can ask questions.

-If you bring in an outside expert, you must pay them! If they are unknown, you should probably pay them $300-$400 for the session, plus travel money. If they are semi-known, it will likely cost you $1,000 a day. If they are nationally known, it is often $5,000 — $20,000 a day. High-end teachers can often be negotiated down (especially if you can help them book other local gigs) but you really shouldn't negotiate the other outside experts' fees down. (This is how they make their living.) And remember, guest preachers should be paid a minimum of $150 — $250 a sermon, plus travel.

-With this in mind, it is acceptable (and possibly advantageous) to charge for the class or seminar. Charging people helps to offset the cost and it communicates to people that you are offering something of *value*. But of course, you don't turn people away who don't have any money. You could simply name a "suggested donation," pass the plate, and inform people (who do not have financial means) that their admission fee is covered.

-Offer childcare for people if you want people with children to attend. (Go hire some baby-sitters.) Depending on your church, you may also want to offer a small meal at your facility.

-Create advertising flyers for people to hand out to friends outside of your church. Put a few in each bulletin and encourage them to invite others. This especially works if you choose a title that seems semi-edgy and/or is based on real life issues and struggles. Advertise it on social media, and inquire about the possibly being interviewed by the local news outlets.

-Have people sign up ahead of time (in the church foyer) and designate a special email address where people can signify that they will be attending. This will help in your preparation, but of course, you would never turn anyone away at the door.

At The Event:
-Make sure that you have plenty of good coffee, make a small plug about your church, and hand all attendees info about your church. Do not waste these kinds of opportunities.

-Be sure to give everyone some "notes" that cover the topic. There is often a longer lasting impact on people if they can leave with a handout that covers the same information that was taught and discussed within the seminar. You will also want to include a list of additional resources they may pursue (other books, podcasts, and the like) and even the contact information of some local counselors, therapists, etc. Our cultural produces very broken people and we will increasingly find people who will need ongoing professional help beyond what the church can offer.

Forming Teams For Mission

Pastors only have so much time, yet new opportunities abound. This section focuses on forming new teams who take on the joy and work of mission.

"At the end of a long day, instead of sending the hungry crowd away, as his disciples came to ask him what to do, Jesus said to them, 'You give them something to eat.' Even though the disciples lacked faith to feed the crowd, Jesus involved them in participating actively in providing food for this huge crowd."

-Orbelina Eguizabal

"Trust is built in the trenches as the team works together, especially on major initiatives."

-Ryan T. Hartwig

"Christ himself gave the apostles, the prophets, the evangelists, the pastors and teachers, to equip his people for works of service."

-Ephesians 4:11-12

Defined:
-In this section, ministry teams are defined *as any group within the church who work together to make ministry happen:* childrens' ministry, youth ministry, social justice projects, Sunday worship, and so on. Building a ministry team is defined *as organizing a group to either: 1) reinvent a ministry or 2) to begin a brand-new initiative.*

Selecting People:
-If your church is putting to a vote who should be on this team, or if the board is making the decision, you are quite likely in trouble. The senior pastor and the staff should be the ones to make these kinds of decisions and to make the personal "asks" for people to be involved. You likely have a better idea of people's gifts and abilities than the board does.

-The most important decision you will make *is who you will ask to be the team leader, or the team point person.* You will want someone who is organized or at least has the skills to deputize someone else to organize, a natural leader whom others follow, and someone who you feel just "gets" the vision of the church. Character obviously matters, but character alone — is not enough for this position. You need someone with some amount of proven leadership ability.

-Additional team members should be solicited who have complimentary gifts to the leader and to each other, *and* who are clearly competent at bringing projects into reality.

-When approaching people about this possibility, make it clear that this will be an *action*-oriented team and not a *decision*-making committee. There is a huge difference between the two. Healthy churches have numerous *teams*. (Groups of people who work together to make something happen.) Unhealthy churches have numerous *decision*-making committees. (Groups of people who get together to talk about what should, or should not, happen.) Do you really want your people investing most of their volunteer time on a committee debating decisions? Or do you want them investing their volunteer time in making things happen?

Your Role With The Team:
-You should consider leading the *first* meeting of the team. Here, you describe the vision of the ministry and the big picture goals, you lay out some basic parameters, and facilitate some initial brainstorming. Once you feel comfortable with their general direction, make sure that they have decided which specific individuals will be responsible for what assignments, and that they have the next meeting scheduled. Remind them that you believe in them and then call it a meeting. After this first meeting, you should *not* personally attend any future meetings unless they are terribly stuck, and they need you to slightly advise them on the best way forward. But that is *all* that you will do: advise and not dictate, advise and not take on tasks personally.

-Check in with the point person every couple of weeks to see how things are going. Play the role of "coach" for them. If they have any problems, use your position to smooth out their road and make their work and ministry as easy as possible. Many times, you will have to offer wise counsel on how to deal with relationship issues on the team. But do your best to not step in unless *absolutely necessary* and do not allow yourself to get "triangled" in the middle of relational difficulties.

-If it's helpful (or if it's needed) provide the team with some articles that may give them some insight into what they are doing. If it is an exceedingly difficult project, you may even need to secure an outside coach to work with the leader.

-When they are ready, have the team leader share on a Sunday morning the team's work and what it all might mean for the church. If they struggle with public-speaking, either work with them ahead of time on what to say. video and edit an announcement, or interview the leader so that you can translate for the congregation their intended message.

-Acknowledge the team, by name, on Sundays for all that they are doing. Brag on them and applaud them publicly. Have the team stand and thank God for them in front of everyone. This will encourage and motivate these team members and will help motivate others to serve within the church.

-Send handwritten notes to the team members thanking them for all that they have done — especially the team leader.

-Once the ministry project is a reality — brag on them again publicly. Make it a meaningful time for the entire congregation. Pray for the team, lay hands on them, tell stories of how it is impacting lives. *This may be the most important thing a pastor does: "making meaning" out of the work of the people.*

-After the project has gone public, meet with the team one more time for a debriefing session. Let the team leader lead — but offer some thoughts, like an outside coach. Choose your words carefully, whatever you say as the pastor has serious weight with others. You *always* want to evaluate ministries once they are up and running and adjust accordingly.

If Things Don't Go Well:
-If you sense that the project isn't going to work: shut it down, or at least delay what they were planning. New initiatives that go public and fail, zap the momentum of a church. It is better to simply cancel the project. You don't have to announce this to everyone. Just provide a few sentences in the bulletin that the plans have been canceled. But meet with the team and thank them for their work and encourage them by admitting that this just happens sometimes.

-If it doesn't go well, personally take the blame and *never* put it on the team. If it goes well, *always* give the team the credit.

What Not To Do:
-See yourself as a "doer" of the project. You are a facilitator, coach,

champion, and occasionally a peace-broker. But never a "doer." If you're a doer, you are holding back the development of the ministry *and* robbing the people of the opportunity to be involved with something meaningful.

-Try not to give them new parameters once they have already begun their work. This will frustrate people beyond belief and they will likely not agree to serve again. Think through the parameters well ahead of time, it is too late to change them later.

Realities:

-No matter how talented the team, there will always be a couple of individuals who do the lion's share of the work. This is regrettable, but not unusual. It's human nature.

-These projects will be a test of how much you trust that the Spirit is working within other people. Can you let go and let them lead this? Do you believe that it is Jesus' church and not yours?

-Ideally, your goal is for all staff and ministry leaders to do what you did here, in their own area of influence: facilitate teams and coach others in doing the ministry. The more leaders you have that can facilitate the ministry (*and not be doers*) the more the ministry will expand, mature, and others' excitement will grow. As a reminder, whenever you are hiring, choose people who organize and facilitate teams, and *not* people who are merely doers.

Celebrating The Church
And Casting Vision

Every non-profit organization has an annual meeting. These events can be transformed into exciting gatherings around vision, instead of boring and contentious business meetings.

"A wise imagination, which is the presence of the spirit of God, is the best guide... for it is not the things we see the most clearly that influence us the most powerfully; undefined, yet vivid visions of something beyond, something which eye has not seen nor ear heard, have far more influence."

-George MacDonald

"Leadership is the capacity to translate vision into reality."

-Warren Bennis

"We had to celebrate and be glad, because this brother of yours was dead and is alive again; he was lost and is found."

-Luke 15:32

Definition And Purpose:
-Every incorporated, non-profit organization is required to hold an *annual meeting*. This is intended to be a public gathering that includes all members, reports on "business," and possibly includes voting on important issues. Although some churches continue to facilitate these gatherings as a typical business meeting, wise leaders often seek to transform them into an inspiring and informative event (that people are excited to attend!) and that still meets legal requirements.

-Traditional church business meetings include the reading of official reports, reading the notes from the previous year's meeting, presenting new business, holding debate or discussion on items and taking a vote.

-The two main problems with traditional church business meetings are:

1. They are incredibly *boring* and only long-term members and

procedure wonks show up for them. (Are churches in a place where they can afford to offer any gathering that is staid and boring?)

2. They can degenerate into serving as magnets for people who want to publicly criticize the church leaders and/or vision. You *must* hold an annual meeting — but there are *so many* more exciting and even potentially life-giving experiences that can be facilitated at these events. There is a better way.

Preparing For An Annual Meeting:

-Obviously, this meeting is held once a year. Most churches hold these meetings at the beginning of a new fiscal year — usually in January or September — depending on when the church's financial calendar begins.

-You will need to compile a print version of an *annual report* to be handed out to every attendee. This is quite an undertaking! You will want to have various leaders write a report on their specific area of the ministry. A helpful practice is to ask them to write the report, send it to you, and then you edit it for clarity and consistency. Many leaders may be unclear as to what they are to write about. Basically, you want them to list highlights or major ministry activities of the year, list plenty of numbers (especially the good ones), and list a few of the major volunteers who have been real contributors. All reports should be no longer than one to two pages.

-Typically, the writer of a ministry report (children, youth, community service, and more) will begin with a couple paragraphs that expresses their excitement about the ministry, their thankfulness for volunteers, and then describe (or even use a bulletpointed list) various highlights from the year. At the end of the report, they will offer a concluding paragraph. "Business" reports: accounting, facility trustees, etc. will write reports that are a little more cut and dried and "numbers crunching" oriented. However, they can still create a short section where they thank others who have been involved.

-You will need reports from *all* ministries: children, youth, small groups, worship team, tech team, community service/social justice, trustees/facilities, accounting, and the church board. You will likely also want the report to include sections on: the official mission and values of the church, the previous years' goals, the goals for the next year(s), attendance figures, membership numbers, baptisms, and proposed budget. All financial accounting should be reported in *detail*. Detailed financial reporting builds trust. Vague financial reporting does not.

-Make it a special evening — don't hold it right after morning worship. Consider either offering a meal or having a potluck dinner beforehand. Your goal is to make this an enjoyable, exciting, and moving meeting. If you plan this event properly, it will motivate people to volunteer more regularly and to move deeper into the life of the church.

-Be sure to plan for childcare, etc. for families. If you don't — they won't come.

-Prepare leaders to only share the "moving stories" from their ministries (when they share before the entire group at the meeting. Not everyone who writes a report needs to share publicly. Only those whose ministries have "clear impact" on others. But you *do* want to have a lot of people share.) These stories should be *well prepared* and selectively chosen. In general, written reports should give all the numbers, figures, and details. Public sharing should stick to the exciting stories. It may also be helpful to have a couple of people share who came to faith in Jesus that year at the church and/or who found real life change. That is what this evening is for. *You are casting vision, creating a culture, and discipling people by how you lead and craft these gatherings.*

At The Actual Meeting:

-Have music playing, proper lighting, and a festive atmosphere when people arrive. Create a sense of anticipation.

-Spend time eating and mingling. Good food and having a good time.

-Open with some music and thanking God in creative ways.

-Have the most "outgoing" member of church leadership host the event and emcee others sharing stories. They can welcome and introduce every leader who shares a story about their ministry. You may even consider having an open mic portion where people share what the Spirit has done in their life of the last year.

-The senior pastor then could share the goals and vision for the next year as well as thanking and acknowledging many people.

-Finally, board members (other than the pastor) should share details about finances and the budget.

-Leave plenty of time for open Q and A. Then hold the vote for the budget (if that is what your church constitution requires).

-Close out with more prayer and worship. Possibly communion?

-If this event is facilitated properly and creatively, people will actually *enjoy* the annual meeting and will be inspired by God's work in the ministry. They will move deeper into the life of the church.

-The art of planning and leading an annual meeting is *not* found in lying about challenging realities or in suppressing what's negative. (You are going to have a time of Q and A after all.) However, it *is* helping people see what God is up to in the church.

Handling Pastoral And Self-Care

Visiting The Sick

All pastors make hospital visits. This entry gives an overview of making them meaningful.

"Do not admire every form of health, and do not condemn every form of illness."

-Gregory of Nazianzus

"A great many of our contemporaries expect that salvation comes from medicine... The physician is a new priest of modern times, a king who holds over them the power of life or death, a prophet of their ultimate destiny."

-Jean-Claude Larchet

"'Lord, when did we see you hungry or thirsty or a stranger or needing clothes or sick or in prison, and did not help you?'

"He will reply, 'Truly I tell you, whatever you did not do for one of the least of these, you did not do for me.'"

-Matthew 25:44-45

Preparing For Hospital Visits:
-You must do enough hospital visits to adequately and tangibly reveal that God loves and remembers the sick, hurting, and dying. If you don't, you'll pay for it. People will begin to feel like you are calloused and uncaring. However, it also hurts your church if you do *too many* hospital visits. You invest much time visiting people, but the ministry as whole, begins to suffer and atrophy. In general, introverts and "driven" pastors can be tempted to neglect hospital visits, while "people-pleasing" pastors tend toward too many. The delicate dance that the pastor must walk is showing adequate concern and care for individuals, while realizing that their role is to oversee the entire ministry of the church.
-You do not need to visit people in the hospital for *anything and everything*. Visits are needed when: it's a life or death event, someone is having a prolonged stay, or if a child or minor is the patient. During

extreme situations (a young person may die from cancer this week, an entire family was in a serious car accident, and similar events) go to the hospital *every day*.

-If anyone ever asks you to visit a friend or family member in the hospital (who are not a part of your church), do it. You are serving the person who is ill *and* their family member who requested your presence.

-Use your time well, try to do several hospital/nursing home visits all in the same trip. All during the same day of the week.

-Take a note pad and pen with you. If the patient is sleeping, or out of their room receiving a test, leave a note at their bed letting them know that you stopped by to see them. This can have the same positive "impact" as actually seeing them personally. If the patient is a child or a minor, always take them a small gift.

-Be sure to dress appropriately — you are going into a professional environment. Even if you lead a casual church, take it up a notch for a hospital visit.

-Check in at the front desk of the hospital when you first arrive. At most hospitals, if you show them your ministry credentials, you can often receive a clergy pass/name badge. This often permits you to visit at any time, often gives you total access to all areas of the hospital, and occasionally grants you free parking.

-Wash your hands thoroughly when you first arrive and brush your teeth and/or use a mint before you leave for the hospital.

-When you arrive at the proper floor, check in at the nurses' station to be sure that the patient can see visitors, find out if there is any special information you need to know, etc. Sometimes, there are instructions posted outside of the patient's room. You may have to go to a special room to scrub up, put on different attire, a mask, and whatever else is needed.

Important Role - But Anything is Possible:
-During a hospital visit, you are playing a *priestly role — you are the physical embodiment of God* to the patient and to the family. Your pastoral presence is more important than who you are as individual, or even, more important than anything that you may say or do while there. A hospital visit from a pastor can be a breath of serious encouragement to the patient and their family.

-However, you must be prepared for *anything*. You never know what may or may not happen during a hospital visit. Sometimes you will be

142

alone with the patient and the visit will be quite personal. Sometimes there may be twenty people packed in a room visiting and you will be playing a very public pastoral role. Sometimes, unintentionally, you will witness people in very vulnerable and revealing states. Sometimes people clam up and barely talk. Sometimes people will be so glad to see you. Sometimes, in grief, people will lash out at you in very unpredictable ways.

"Typical" Hospital Visit:

-Look for any special signs/medical protocols listed on the door of the patient. You might be required to wear a mask, a robe, or take some other precaution. If the directions are confusing, ask a nurse or another medical professional before entering the room.

-Be sure to knock before you enter their room or announce your presence vocally if they are behind a curtain. People are in all sorts of vulnerable situations in a hospital and you do not want to surprise them.

-During a typical visit:

-*Be fairly cheery and positive* (part of your job is to be encouraging)

-*Ask them, "How are you doing today?"*

-*Listen empathetically*

-*Spend time in small talk* (they are likely bored or looking for a distraction)

-*Read a passage of scripture to them and pray for them* (while laying hands on them be sure to "touch" them)

-*Ask them if they need anything — a magazine, a book, etc. (if so- go get it for them) and let them know to contact you if they need anything else*

-*Fifteen to twenty minutes is usually a sufficient visit* (if this is not a life or death situation)

Odds and Ends:

-If some medical professional walks in the room during the visit, offer to step outside — this avoids putting the patient in an awkward position.

-However, be prepared to see anything: some may be unkempt, even barely dressed, and yet still welcome you into their room.

-Do not offer false promises or tell stories of people in a similar situation that ended *negatively*.

-You may have to be strong for other family members and even possibly mediate between them and the hospital.

-Be very careful in offering any medical advice, but if they have been in the hospital for a long time and are not getting better — you may suggest that they consider a different specialist or hospital. It will help you to have some working knowledge of various hospitals' strengths and weaknesses within the region. In today's world, the patient must advocate for themselves. Hospitals and physicians do not do this for patients. Many people do not seem to understand this situation. You may need to help play this role for them.

Crisis Situations:

-In a real crisis, stay with the patient/family until the situation is resolved... *or* the family suggests you go home (they often say "thank-you for coming.") However, never leave someone in the waiting room by themselves during a crisis moment.

-Pray with the family, small talk with them, offer to buy them lunch.

-But in general, simply *be present* as people are worried, grieving, there are no magic words, simply *be present*.

Weddings That Work

Performing wedding ceremonies has the potential to not only bless the bride and groom, but also, to make a favorable impression on their friends and family. Here, well organized and highly personal ceremonies are covered.

"The sexes are two stubborn pieces of iron; if they are to be welded together, it must be while they are red-hot. Every woman has to find out that her husband is a selfish beast, because every man is a selfish beast by the standard of a woman. But let her find out the beast while they are both still in the story of 'Beauty and the Beast.' Every man has to find out that his wife is cross — that is to say, sensitive to the point of madness: for every woman is mad by the masculine standard. But let him find out that she is mad while her madness is more worth considering than anyone else's sanity."

-G.K. Chesterton

"The eschaton is often compared to a wedding, the wedding of the lamb with the church. And if you are like me, and have been to a few weddings, that metaphor is kind of depressing. Our modern American ceremonies don't seem to capture the eschatological joy the biblical writers were aiming for."

-Richard Beck

"The Lord God said, 'It is not good for the man to be alone.'"

-Genesis 2:18

Before Agreeing To The Ceremony:
-Check with the appropriate department of the state in which the wedding is to be performed to inquire if you need to fill out a license to perform a wedding ceremony.
-Assuming you want to marry the couple, be clear and upfront with them about the process, before they make a final decision to have you officiate the ceremony. Discuss payment ($300 to $500, paid on

145

the wedding day, pro-bono for those with limited means), counseling sessions, and dates. Require them to give you the marriage license at the rehearsal, or you will not perform the wedding ceremony.

Pre-marital Counseling (In Preparation For The Ceremony)

-Use your final pre-marital session to plan the ceremony. Bring a blank or standard ceremony to the meeting and allow them to add to it, remove things, or change the order. Most people enjoy a somewhat traditional ceremony but now and then you will have someone who wants to break all the rules. It is their wedding, not yours, do what they want. It may be helpful to gently remind them that their parents may have certain expectations. They do not have to do what their parents are expecting, but they must be prepared for the consequences.

-Inquire: about their wedding colors and what they are expecting you to wear to the ceremony and to the rehearsal; that they have back-up plans for inclement weather (if the ceremony is held outdoors), that you will need to be mic-ed; that they have a "coordinator" who will assist you during the rehearsal and the ceremony; that everyone who will be in the ceremony will be at the rehearsal; that all music is either live, or can be "looped" for extra time; and so on.

-Take half an hour and ask them about them: where they grew up, how they met, how the proposal took place, what they do for a living, what they have in common, what are their differences, what music or movies they enjoy, funny stories they remember, how they would describe each other, and take extensive notes. Make sure you get the details right. You will use these for your wedding homily. It's fine to let them know this is what you are doing.

Rehearsal:

-The week of the ceremony, go over your notes in preparing for the ceremony and write out exactly what needs to happen in extensive detail. No detail should be missed. If you don't know something, call or text the couple and find out before the rehearsal. Your goal is to come in with complete knowledge of everything (where flowers will be, where the soloist will sing from, where you will stand during the solo) before the rehearsal.

-Write your homily — weaving details of their story with a biblical passage or narrative. Write this out word for word. You don't want to get any of this wrong.

146

-Print your detailed wedding notes (should be several pages) and take them with you to the rehearsal.

Wedding Rehearsal And Ceremony:
-Arrive thirty minutes early for the rehearsal to be sure you know where everyone will stand, where the bridal party enters and exits. Go over any questions you still have with the couple.

-Gather everyone together and introduce yourself and the wedding coordinator. Have the couple introduce all their friends and family who are there. Let them know you are excited for the wedding, but it's time to get serious at the rehearsal. Clearly communicate that no one is to offer their opinions on the ceremony unless the bride and groom ask for them. You are playing the heavy here so that the couple does not have to.

-Begin with everyone standing in place as if the bride has just walked down the aisle. Make sure everyone is in the right location and have the coordinator "eye it up" and use a piece of tape to make everyone's spot - to assure that everyone is evenly spaced.

-Quickly go through the ceremony — not reading everything, just enough that everyone knows what to say and where to go and when. Remind everyone involved to look at you if confused during the ceremony. You will be the field general who will guide everyone if they become confused. Then practice the recessional and its timing.

-Afterward, have everyone go to where they will be before the ceremony begins — including mothers who are being seated. Have them practice the recessional with music, timing, and so on. Then again, walk through the ceremony, and have them go through the recessional.

-Practice them coming in one more time and then call it a night.

-Remind everyone this is to be an enjoyable weekend. However, something will go wrong — just expect it. Don't anticipate a perfect day.

Wedding Day:
-On the day of the ceremony, arrive at least thirty minutes early and check with the coordinator and make sure everything is set.

-And then go!!!

Wedding Service Outline

-Are groomsmen also ushers? (Are they seating guests on bride and groom sides?)

-Formal Seating Order: grandparents... groom's parents... bride's parents...

-Men walk in - (grasp their hands in front or back?)

Processional (flower girl and ring bearer)... and then the ladies enter...

Nod for Mother to stand

Welcome and Brief Pastoral Prayer

"Welcome to this great occasion..."

(Flower girl/ ring bearer sit during the prayer.)

"Please be seated."

Giving of the Bride

Who is giving this woman to be married to this man?

Bride's father answers, *"Her Mother and I."*

Bride hands her flowers to the maid of honor, maid of honor hands hers to the other bridesmaid- (time to talk if want to)

Vows of Intention (traditional- ends with "I will")

-Charge to the groom: **Before the omniscient God, and in the presence of these witnesses, will you, John Allen Smith, take Joan Anne Jones, here present, to be your wedded wife? Will you love and comfort her, honor and keep her, and in joy and sorrow, preserve with her this bond, holy and unbroken, forsaking all others, striving to keep a pure mind and body only unto her, so long as you both shall live? If so, answer,** *I will*.

-Charge to the bride: (same as above)

Scripture Reading/Poetry Reading.

Pastoral Homily

Exchanging of Vows

They turn and face one another

Groom's vows: **John, please repeat after me. "I, John, take you, Joan, to be my to be my wedded wife. // and, I promise before God and these witnesses to be your loving and faithful husband;// to have and to hold from this day forward;// for better or worse; for richer and or poorer;// in sickness and in health; to love and to cherish; 'til death do us part. // according to God's holy love, I pledge you my trust."**

Bride's vows: (same as above)

Presentation of rings

John and Joan, you have chosen rings as a symbol of your pledge. The ring is very fitting as the sign of the marriage union. The circle speaks of that which is eternal and unending, a picture of God's unending love for each another. Your rings are made of precious metal, tested and proven pure. Our prayer for you, is that your love will prove true in the test of time as pure gold does in fire.

- Reach over and get the rings from best man

- Groom's ring vows: **I give you this ring as a symbol of my vow/// and with all that I am, and all that I have, I honor you.**

- Bride's ring vows: (same)

Solo? Rose Ceremony? Family Prayer? Communion? Unity Candle? Any other additions?

(They return and hold hands facing each other.)

Brief pastoral prayer - (Flower girl and ring bearer join the bridal party)

Pronouncement of marriage (kiss the bride)

Inasmuch as you, John, and you, Joan, have consented to marry each other and have witnessed the same before God and these family and friends, by virtue of the authority vested in me as a minister of the word of God, and by the laws of the state of…., I do now pronounce you husband and wife, united in the pure and holy bonds of wedlock, and those whom God has joined together, let no man put asunder.

You may now kiss your bride!

Benediction-

Now to him who is able to do immeasurably more than all we ask or imagine, according to his power that is at work within us, to him be glory in the church and in Christ Jesus throughout all generations, for ever and ever! Amen.

Presentation of couple

- Maid of honor hands flowers back to the bride

And now, may I present to you, Mr. and Mrs. John and Joan Smith.

-Bride and groom leave

-Bridal party leaves

-Parents' leave

Counseling For Life And Marriage

Pastoral counseling can change someone's life or drive them from the church and from God. A crash overview of wise counsel is explored.

"Understand, then, if you can, what the pilgrimages of the soul are especially when it laments with groaning and grief... When the soul has returned to its rest, that is, to the homeland of paradise, it will be taught more truly and it will understand more truly the meaning of what the pilgrimage was."

-Origen

"The personal costs of counseling also remind us why it is so necessary for a counselor to experience continuous renewal through Scripture, prayer, and the sacraments. Only when one's own spiritual batteries are being continuously recharged can one hope to have something to give to others. And only in one's own personal walk with the Lord can one find the strength to bear not only one's own burdens but also those of others."

-David G. Benner

"Confess your sins to each other and pray for each other so that you may be healed."

-James 5:16

Counseling:
General Thoughts:
-People do not come to pastors for counseling quite as much today as they used to. In general, less educated and traditional people seek out pastors. Professionals and progressives seek out therapists. However, if your preaching and leading comes across as rather human and authentic, more people will come to you for counsel. People want to talk with those who seem wise, have a valuable opinion, and who are accepting and understanding of ordinary human beings and their struggles.
-Your basic goals are:

1. That the individual feels heard and cared for. Most people have no one to simply share their secrets and struggles with.

2. To offer a sense of meaning and purpose amid struggle, combining their problems with the Christian narrative.

3. That people leave with hope, not the false hope that things will work out as they desire necessarily, but that God is with them and things will not always be like this.

4. Offer some practical actions that they can take. This does not mean, again, that everything will be "fixed", but that there is something that they can do. Taking some sort of action is a crucial part of people dealing with difficult situations and seasons. It can be quite depressing for a person in a difficult situation if there are not any actions that they can take to bring even a modicum of relief.

How To Prepare Yourself For Pastoral Counseling:

-You must have been through counseling yourself and have read plenty of psychology or you will be severely limited as a counselor. Psychology is not the gospel, but it does provide you with a more nuanced understanding of the human experience.

-You must be a person of prayer and meditation, to be personally familiar with how God works, or you will be severely limited as a counselor. This is not the same thing as being well-versed theologically.

-You must keep growing or you will be limited as a counselor.

What To Do:

-Sit in a welcoming posture, next to the counselee and not in a power position (like behind a desk.) You are primarily *listening* to them. People long to be heard within a context of love and acceptance. This *alone* can be rather life changing.

-Hopefully, you can offer them a sense of *perspective* — to help them understand if their situation is *uniquely* serious or if it a rather *common* struggle.

- Offer people a few "practical" handles — help create an action plan for them. It is living hell to be in pain and not have any kind of plan of how to deal with it. Perhaps offer a book to read, a local therapist to see, another person in the church that they can talk to, or a support group to visit. The church may need to offer to help finance some of this.

-Pray for them. You are representing God to them during this struggle.

-Check in with them (a simple phone call, email, or text) within a week or so to see how they are doing.

What Not To Do:
-Simply drop everything to see someone *immediately*. Have them schedule an appointment. Otherwise, you are training people to expect you to always be immediately available and you and the church *will* suffer in the long run.

-See people for *multiple* sessions. This is not your training, it is unlikely that they will find deep life-change with you, and you will neglect many other important tasks in the church. This does not tend to help anyone. If someone is dealing with a complex situation that requires ongoing counsel, it is likely more helpful for them if you would refer them to a trusted licensed Christian therapist.

-Naively trust *their interpretation* of their situation (but do trust their *experience*). The real problem is rarely what they immediately believe that it is.

-Take sides in a relational dispute and assume that the one who came to you is truly the innocent party.

-Offer simple answers — *they do not exist*. Every possible action (even good ones) have negative trade-offs.

-Be confident that you have answers for them. It is completely fine to say, *"I don't know how to help you."*

Pre-marital Counseling:
-Before you agree to marry a couple, require them to see a family counselor/therapist for a few sessions. Primarily it should focus on family of origin, individual backstories, and personality issues. Base your decision, to marry them or not, based on the report of the counselor/therapist. This gives you a pair of outside eyes and ears and takes you personally out of the messy situation of possibly suggesting that a couple not marry.

-Require the couple to meet with you for pre-marital counseling. Typically three to four sessions are adequate. This can be completed "one on two" or with a few different couples if you are marrying several during the same season. You could assign them a book to read and discuss it together, have them complete a workbook and go over their assignments with you, or simply engage them in conversation. The whole point of pastoral pre-marital counseling is to discuss areas that may become complicated *after* they are married. If they have discussed these ahead of time, they will be less shaken when these issues come to the surface in real life. Because they *will* come up. The main issues you will want to discuss include: family background and in-law tensions (little things tend to become big things), finances and goals for the future, and how they communicate and deal with their different personalities. There are the main issues for couples parrying today. You do not need to be the "answer" person (those days are gone), but ask many questions and get them discussing areas of tension. Being an avid reader of psychology and family therapy will assist you greatly in this process.

-Use your final pre-marital session to plan the ceremony. Bring a blank or standard ceremony to the meeting and allow them to add to it, remove things, and/or change the order. Most people enjoy a fairly traditional ceremony, but now and then you will have someone who wants to break all the rules! It is their wedding, not yours, do what *they* want.

-Inquire: about their wedding colors and what they are expecting you to wear to the ceremony and to the rehearsal; that they have "back-up" plans for inclement weather (if the ceremony is taking place outside), that you will be mic-ed; that they have some type a "coordinator" who will assist you during the rehearsal and the ceremony, that everyone who will be in the ceremony will be at the rehearsal, that all music is either live, or that it can be "looped" for extra time.

-Take half an hour and ask them about *them*: where they grew up, how they met, how the proposal took place, what they do for a living, what they have in common, what are their differences, what music or movies they enjoy, funny stories they remember, and how they would describe each other. Take extensive notes on what they tell you. Make sure that you get the details right. You will use these for your wedding homily — to make it personal and special for them. It's fine to let them know this is what you are doing.

Making Meaning At Memorials
For The Deceased

Few things are more intimidating for the inexperienced pastor than their first funeral. This section provides advice to limit pastoral fear and to bless grieving family members.

"When we think of death and dying today, one of the first things that comes to mind is the fact that, for the most part, death has been removed from the ordinary experience of most people in our culture. It is true that we see death over and over on the evening news reports, but it is always distant and does not involve people who are close to us."

-Zachary Hayes

"Grace, as God's self-communication, presents death not as a punishment, but as a two-sided opportunity: intensifying the relationship between the human person and God. One is called to die every day in the name of one's neighbor. At the same time, this selfless act culminates in powerless submission before the presence of God, at the final end of life."

-Julito Paraguya

"We do not want you to be uninformed about those who sleep in death, so that you do not grieve like the rest of mankind, who have no hope. For we believe that Jesus died and rose again, and so we believe that God will bring with Jesus those who have fallen asleep in him."

-1 Thessalonians 4:13-14

Being Prepared For Unplanned
-If you are dealing with fears of death, dead bodies, or other related areas, set up a tour of a local funeral home. This will likely help you. You do not want to be working through this at a funeral that you are officiating!

-No one ever dies at a convenient time — stay ahead of your church/ministry work. If you have put off what you need to do for Sunday and someone dies unexpectantly, that is your fault. These things tend to feel like they come all at once. Be prepared for *anything*. Especially with an unexpected and sudden death. Everyone handles grief and tragedy differently and how people respond can be rather unpredictable. This is *not* the time to get on your hobbyhorse as to "how" people should act immediately after a sudden death. In shocking and difficult seasons, and recognizing that there are biological factors that help determine people's responses, let people respond however they respond.

Meeting With Family Immediately After The Death:
-As much as we believe in the priesthood of all believers, during this time, you are playing the role of *the priest*. You represent God to people. Your calm, encouraging, and caring presence is *everything*.

-This is not a time to try to offer people "answers" about tragedies and death, even if they ask for some! (If they truly want to process these issues — there will be time for this a few weeks later. Sometimes, after a month or two, they will no longer have a desire to discuss these matters.) Simply be *present*, and *listen* to people, and *pray* with them, and *hug* them. This is a ministry of *presence* and *personal touch* and not theological formulations.

-People should be (and should be encouraged to be) talking and crying quite a bit. Stoicism is concerning. If people are *not* talking and mourning, this should alert you to a potential problem.

-Never say *"I know how you feel."* A simple *"I am very sorry... May I pray for you?"* is sufficient. These are good times for "high-touch" with others. Even with people who are not typically inclined to such experiences. Take the initiative. They often need it.

-*Never* leave a widow or widower home by themselves at night, right after a spouse has died. Arrange for one of their friends or family members or a church member to stay at their home with them. If you cannot find someone — you should stay with them.

-Depending on the situation and the family — sometimes you need to be the cool-headed person who steps in and organizes arrangements for people: transportation and a place to stay for out of town family, getting meals organized, and so on. It really helps if you have a team of people at the church who are prepped to lead in these times. Get forming that team — complete with thought-through instructions for them. Remember — *your job is to equip people for ministry*. Sometimes this means that you take the time, ahead of time, to create "guide sheets"

155

for church people to serve others during these seasons. If you do your homework, and really think this through, your church will be able to truly bless hurting people and they will avoid potential "landmines" that assumptions made in the moment, without predetermined plans, can often create.

-When people say, *"Thanks for coming"* that means it is time to go home.

Meeting With The Family To Plan The Memorial:

-Sometimes you go to the funeral home with the family (not always) — ask them if they would like you to attend. Be prepared (if need be) to help them make decisions. In general, the cheaper, the better. Grieving people do not always see this. They believe that they are somehow honoring the dead by spending more money than they should.

-Ask many questions about the deceased and write all the details down: their life as a child, major accomplishments, career, hobbies, positive qualities, funny memories, significant dates, names and details of family members. The family should be giving you plenty of "positive" material, but also possibly a few of their foibles. Some details may be found in the official obituary.

-Encourage the family to make picture collages, (possibly a video), of the deceased for the memorial. This can be very helpful in processing experiences of grief.

-Encourage people to share about the deceased at the memorial service. It is best if you can get a couple of people lined up (ahead of time) who are willing to share and then have a period of open mic afterward. If some people are not prepared ahead of time to share — it is likely that no one will (because no likes to be first). This can be rather awkward at a memorial service — no one sharing personally about the deceased.

-Encourage people (but do not insist) to allow children to attend the memorial service. Many want to shelter children from mourning, but it is most often better for children if they know what is happening and are a part of the day. However, this decision should finally be made by their parents.

-Attend the viewing, but do not feel you should be there the entire time. Usually the beginning and ending is sufficient. You cannot drop everything else in church ministry when someone dies!

Preparing For The Service:

-What you are doing is "meaning-making" of the life of the deceased. Bring Jesus in for a mash-up with their life.

-The eulogy should combine scripture, mainly the "good parts" of the deceased's life, and yet include some realism about who they were. Be mainly positive, yet don't overdo it. Tie their life into the life of Jesus narratively.

-Be very careful about bringing in heaven and hell. Handle that very *carefully*.

-Bring in a humorous story or two about the deceased to break the tension, but not *too* many.

-If they died in tragic or unnatural circumstances (suicide, overdose, murder, and so on) you are going to have to *go there*. Not with a theology of the "issue" but that this is "not what God intended" — give voice to the pain people are experiencing.

-At the funeral or memorial service: Once it is over, you (as priest) walk at the head of the casket and lead it out to the hearse and stand there until the door of the hearse is shut.

-At the graveside/committal service: Walk to the hearse (before they unload the casket) and lead the casket all the way to the grave. You are the last person to walk away from the graveside.

Memorial Service Outline
(Your Part Should Be No More Than Twenty Minutes)

Instrumental Music
Opening Scripture Reading
Prayer
Obituary- (often officially reading the official obituary — maximum three to four minutes)
    -Where deceased was born and raised
    -Major benchmarks in their life — graduated high school and college, when married, birth of children, and so on
    -Any significant contributions: employment, community service, plus more
Solo or Congregational Singing?
Eulogy/ Message
Personal Sharing From Others (prep some people ahead of time —

depending on the person or group — this could go one for a long time. In general, let people share, but at rather large memorials, you may have to cut it off after ample sharing.)

Congregational Singing or Instrumental Music

Closing Prayer

Dismiss Guests (while family remains)

Committal Service

Brief Scripture Reading

Brief Comments to the Family (widow/widower, children) — Only a paragraph or two. Comments of support, family and friends are there for them.

Prayer

Opportunity for family members to drop roses on the casket

Offering Peace To New Parents

Having a baby is exciting and scary. If churches can care for new parents through this process, they can offer a sign of God's love and often ensure that emerging families make a home there.

"For those who love Jesus and want to glorify him, it's embarrassing to admit feeling overwhelmed by the children God gave us. When new moms hear messages from the church like 'Do not fear,' 'Do not to be overwhelmed,' and 'Trust God,' it's easy to worry that admitting any struggles may be perceived as sinful, faithless, or reflect a lack of gratitude for what God's given."

-Lindsey Carlson

"The problem: spiritual hopelessness in the face of utter exhaustion and a depletion of resources."

-Tania Geist

"Carry each other's burdens, and in this way you will fulfill the law of Christ."

-Galatians 6:2

-Giving birth to a child (especially the first child) is an exciting time for the parents, but also a very difficult one. It takes the healthiest and most well-adjusted parents a good six weeks to adjust to a new routine, a lack of sleep, even a new familial and personal identity. For many people the transition takes much, much longer.

-If the church can offer proper and welcomed support, the family will make a smoother transition and form deep bonds with their local Christian community.

Preparing for the Birth:
-At times, people will confide in you before anyone else at the church that they are expecting a child. Whenever someone shares this, be super excited for them. Sometimes, this becomes old hat for you, or maybe you don't know them overly well, and so you are not necessarily

overwhelmed with personal excitement. But this is exciting for them, and since you represent the church and Jesus to them, you should at least *act* excited. However, keep this to yourself. Don't spoil their opportunity to share their excitement by you sharing it with others. The only exception may be your spouse. They likely will expect you to share it with them. But your spouse must also keep it under wraps and yet, quickly reach out to the expecting couple and let them know that they are excited for them.

-Having women at the church throw a baby shower is huge. Even if their friends and family are already doing so, it means a lot to the expecting mother. Someone needs to do the legwork to figure out what they truly need. Offering needed gifts makes it so much more meaningful.

-If the expecting mother is rather poor, do everything to lavish gifts on the family.

-If the expecting mother is a teenager or unwed, do your best to still show proper excitement and be sure to throw a baby shower. Many are expecting the church to be judgmental and reject the expecting mother in this kind of situation. This is a tremendous opportunity to lead your church in seeing the value of loving and accepting all people and to be truly pro-life in the best sense of the word. There is absolutely no need for you to voice any kind of disapproval. You may also want to recruit some seasoned mothers, who are full of grace, to especially come around the expecting mother to mentor her, encourage her, and help carry some of the struggle for her.

-Ask the expecting couple to let you know when the baby is born, even if it is by text message. Many people today will just assume that you knew the child was born. You will want to be in the know.

Once the child is born:

-Find out if the parents would appreciate visitors at the hospital, or at home, or if they would prefer having some space. This can tremendously vary, typically based on the personality of the mother. Some moms want everyone to come to the hospital right away and see the baby. Others prefer to go into hiding and do not want anyone to visit them at all. This cannot be predicted ahead of time. Most mothers have, at least temporarily, a "personality change" for a season after giving birth. Always ask and never assume.

-If the new mother is a staff member or board member (or wife of one), or if she is single or a teenager, make sure that you personally visit her and the baby in the hospital. This will communicate a lot to them. If the mother is simply a typical married member of the church, you do not need to personally visit them in the hospital.

-Be sure to announce the birth in the church bulletin, at their small group, or wherever is appropriate. But unless they requested visitors (which is rather rare) let people know to not call them or visit them. However, encourage people to send them cards — especially cards that contain gift cards to department stores, restaurants, and the like.

-A crucially important way to serve these families is to appoint one person to organize meals for the family. This cannot be overstated.

-Have the point person contact the family ahead of time and find out what kinds of food they like or do not like or if there are any food allergies. They should also find out the best time for people to bring over meals. The goal should be for people to bring them over a meal on Mondays, Wednesdays, and Fridays for two to three weeks.

-The coordinator should then reach out to different people and ask them to either make the family a meal and deliver it, or to order take out and to deliver it to the home. Additionally, they need to ask everyone what they are expecting to take to the family to assure it fits their tastes and that there is proper variety. It is a "waste" to bring them meals that they don't enjoy or if everyone brings them the same dish.

-All meals are to be delivered in disposable containers. It is a huge pain for new parents to have to track, whose dishes are whose, and to try to get them back to people.

-People are instructed to not stick around when they bring a meal. Deliver it and leave. Unless the mother asks them to stick around and see the baby.

-Finally, the meal coordinator should provide the final schedule of meals to the family so that they know what to expect, and when, and from whom.

-If they have other children, it may be a real blessing if other families would volunteer to take their other children for a day, overnight, on weekends, or whenever. Parents of multiple children, when they have a new baby, rarely get sleep and this is a huge blessing to them.

-If the baby is born with a serious condition and will be in the hospital for some time, you should visit the family right away and you or a staff member from the church should visit every few days or so. Prayer and meals should be organized for the new parents and childcare for other children if needed.

-Note: Some new parents do not seem to have the resources to handle a new addition very easily. It is quite common for new parents to completely check out of church for quite a while. If they do, find ways to stay in contact with them so that they do not feel forgotten.

Dealing With Difficult Situations

Every church contains their share of situations that are thorny and painful. Though there are not any decisive answers, there are ways of healthily managing these dicey seasons.

"The degree of pain we are experiencing at any time almost always includes two variables: the stimulus 'causing' the discomfort, and the threshold for tolerance — that is, the capacity to overcome or perhaps reduce the sensation itself."

-Edwin H. Friedman

"What is the good of telling you about my feelings? You know them already: they are the same as yours. I am not arguing that pain is not painful. Pain hurts. That is what the word means. I am only trying to show that the old Christian doctrine of being made 'perfect through suffering' is not incredible. To prove it palatable is beyond my design."

-C.S. Lewis

"We have this treasure in jars of clay to show that this all-surpassing power is from God and not from us. We are hard pressed on every side, but not crushed; perplexed, but not in despair; persecuted, but not abandoned; struck down, but not destroyed. We always carry around in our body the death of Jesus, so that the life of Jesus may also be revealed in our body."

-1 Corinthians 4:7-10

General Personal Instructions:
-It is vital that you do everything you can (engaging spiritual disciplines, seeing a therapist, getting sleep and taking care of yourself) to be in a good place *personally* because you will never know when a crisis is going to hit. They tend to come at the most inconvenient times! How you will handle these situations, and how you will care for people, will largely be based on your personal health and maturity. You cannot make up for this during a crisis, how you will handle difficult situations

is pre-determined by how much investment you have been making in your soul and person long before the presenting events.

-When people first share with you about any type of sudden crisis, it is vital that you personally stay calm. As the senior leader of the church, you will set the tone for how the church reacts. If you fall apart, so will they. This does not mean that you are to be a pillar of stoicism — share your concern for those involved, that you are sorry for what they are going through, etc. But you cannot lose it emotionally. Tears? Yes. Overwhelmed? No — at least not in front of those whom you serve.

-Reach out to an older, veteran pastor for personal counsel. This is invaluable. You will want a seasoned person's advice in handling this type of situation.

-If it is a severe enough crisis, notify your denominational superior. They often have some level of legal liability invested in your church. Keep them in the loop on the front end.

-Remember, it is not your job to fix everything and make everything better. This is God's job, not yours. Your job is to (as wisely as possible) lead the church to an appropriate response and to serve as the public face of the church during the crisis. However, try to resist the urge to spend all your time on the presenting crisis for days on end. Many times, anything more than a couple of hours a day on this issue will not lead to any improvement in the situation. If you focus only on the crisis, the rest of the church will be neglected (your sermons, other meetings, other people, and more) and the ministry will begin to suffer if you become consumed with this one matter. This will make everything worse.

-If this is an ongoing crisis, or a season of real struggle, personally see a counselor (to deal with your anxiety) and lean on some friends *outside of the church*. You may even want to schedule some time to see a friend outside of the church to simply have fun and let your hair down. You will need this. Periods of prolonged stress raises your cortisol levels and eventually will make you physically ill — if you do not get some help or find some outlets where you can share and unwind.

Discerning The Difference Between An Urgent/ Serious Matter And A True Crisis:

-Ascertaining which is which is very important. If you treat "serious" matters like a "crisis" you will quickly burn out and you will reveal yourself to be too inexperienced, or too immature, to lead a church. You may lose credibility over time and you will foster an unstable church culture. If you treat "crises" only like "serious" matters you will at the very least be labeled as aloof, and possibly even as legally negligent.

-Examples Of Possibly Urgent/Serious Matters (But Ones That Are Not A Crisis):
-a church member loses their job
-a church member leaves their spouse
-a church member's child gets arrested
-an older church member dies
-personal conflict with a staff member
-a church member is hospitalized
-a church member denies the faith

-Examples Of True Crisis Situations:
-a church staff member has an affair or suddenly files for divorce
-an accusation of abuse of a child within the church
-the sudden and unexpected death of a younger church member
-a severe accident at a church event
-a fatal or life altering accident involving a church member
-a young person is diagnosed with cancer
-negative public press about your church
-sudden, disgruntled resignation of a staff member
-child of a church member runs away
-suicide of a church member

Handling The Situation As The Leader Of An Organization:
-If this is a matter that could impact the entire church, or if it is a legitimate safety matter, notify your church board and your staff of the situation. Remind them that they serve the church by keeping this as a private matter until everyone figures how to respond.

-Depending on the situation, notify your church's insurance company right away and possibly seek legal counsel.

-Share with the church everything that you can legally on a Sunday morning. Spend adequate time thinking through your words so that you cannot be accused of saying something that you did not intend to. This could be during Sunday worship or could be in a meeting for members after worship. This way, only regulars and those "in the know" will show up for the meeting. You will want the board to stand up front with you and possibly speak on the matter as well. This should not be your crisis to bear alone.

-In some situations, you may need to send a snail mail letter to the homes of all the church's members. Make sure your board approves the draft before you send it and craft the letter to be sent from the entire board and not just from you.

Caring For Church Members Directly Involved In The Crisis:
-Go and meet with them as soon as possible. Be a calming influence without offering false hope. Lay hands on them and pray for them. In some situations, you may want to take other staff or board members along with you. Stay with them at this initial meeting as long as they need you. It may be a long night.

-Pastorally lead those affected by creating a practical plan of action for them as they deal with the crisis. Many times, people are in shock and are not thinking clearly and you will need to guide them into prudent courses of action. Clearly, this does not mean that you have a "plan" that can make everything better. But people do need a practical plan of "what they can do" to give them a measure of hope.

-Check in with them by phone, at least every other day. In some situations, you may need to personally visit them every week.

-Find a counselor or therapist for the individual or the family. Have the church pay for it if needed.

-Organize a lay-led team (hopefully this is already in place) for people to make meals for the family, clean their house, do their laundry, grocery shop for them, visit them in the hospital or at home, and more. Designate a point leader for this team — one person that they can call or text with any needs, at any hour. This team will likely need to proactively care for the family. Many people will not admit that they have needs when they truly do. The team should simply care for the hurting whether asked for it or not. When people are "fine" — they will usually let you know as the pastor.

-You may need to tap the benevolence fund of the church to help people out financially.

-Depending on the situation, you may need to arrange for a safe place for them to stay, or even create a safety plan for the entire church. If in anyway someone feels unsafe, encourage them to call the police.

-With permission, pray for family members during Sunday worship, laying hands on them, as they are surrounded by lay people. These can be powerful and healing times.

Loving Complex People, While Also Leading The Entire Church

Jesus calls us to welcome and love everyone. At the same time, some people's lives are so complex, that for the sake of the entire church, they need to be handled with real wisdom and special care.

"At the cross, Jesus subjects himself to disability, and his resurrected body continues to bear his scars as a sign of God's solidarity with humanity."

-Thomas E. Reynolds

"By embracing the 'outcast,' Jesus underscored the 'sinfulness' of the persons and systems that cast them out."

-Miroslav Volf

"'Truly I tell you, whatever you did for one of the least of these brothers and sisters of mine, you did for me.'"

-Matthew 25:40

The Delicate Balance:
-Here we come upon another aspect of pastoral ministry that requires a real balancing act: on one hand, you are nurturing a community of faith that is open to everyone and extends grace and forgiveness to all people. On the other hand, you are the leader of a non-profit organization and you need to protect the legal liability of the church. This is always a fine line to walk.

-If specific situations pop up in which you need board feedback, but believe you cannot betray personal conversations, talk about the situation with your board with the individual remaining unnamed as you all try to decide the best way forward.

Ex-Offenders:
-Plain and simple: people with a prison record cannot serve with teens or children. This may not be fair in every circumstance, but if

anything were to happen and people knew that you knew about their past, you will likely be fired, and your church could be successfully sued.

-If someone is a registered sex-offender, besides not being able to serve with children and youth, you should have a direct conversation with them. Let them know that you believe that there is room for them in the community and that God loves them. But also let them know that you need to notify your church board and staff about their background. Assure them that this isn't trying to smear them, but for legal reasons, others need to be in the know. If they cannot agree to this- they cannot attend your church. Additionally, be sure that they are continuing to see their therapist or caseworker.

-On the plus side, when you talk with your board and staff about this individual, besides covering appropriate protocols, you can help them to see that Jesus makes room for everyone in his church, no matter what they may have done in the past. The community of Jesus is open to everyone.

The Mentally Ill:
-If you find out that someone has been diagnosed with a serious mental illness (and one that can impact other people), you need to keep this quiet unless it may directly involve others: they are asked to help with children, serve in a major leadership capacity, etc. The ill church member should know (ahead of time) if you need to have a conversation with others about their struggles. But this is rarely necessary. If there is not real potential that their illness could directly impact people within the church- nothing should be said.

-In all actuality, you will often only become aware of their mental illness if they experience episode or breakdown at a public church event.

-In general, view their condition similarly to how you see a physical issue. Some people cannot walk without assistance, others need to take heart medication, others may need psychiatric medications and regular therapy.

-Never encourage someone that they are "cured" and no longer need to see a psychiatrist or take medication. *Never.*

-If need be, you may be able to discuss their condition with their professional caretaker if they give the professional permission to talk with you. This may be helpful in creating a health plan for them and/or inquiring about their ability to serve in certain roles within the church.

Needy People:

-Needy people are those poor souls who seem to have a weekly crisis, who go on and on about their personal problems with everyone in the church nearly every week, and who call you consistently wanting to see you and talk with you about their struggles. For our discussion, these are people who seem to "seek out trouble" and no matter what you or the church does for them, they almost refuse to pull out of crisis mode. I am not referring to people who are amid a serious crisis and who truly need immediate help.

-Do your best to not allow this individual to personally pull you into their drama. This will drain you, lead you to neglecting the church over time, and often, will not benefit the needy individual very much. Instead, connect them with a group of people, who together, can share some of the load in caring for them. However, this team will need some training and guidance.

-It is crucial that leaders, such as their small group leader be given instruction and permission to "re-direct matters" when they try to take over the group, sharing Their personal struggles. Few people attend a small group when one person seems to take it over every week.

-The best thing you can do for these individuals is often to help them create a plan. Attending a small group, spiritual practices to implement, or a therapist to see. If need be, pay for a few therapy sessions for them.

-Sometimes it is also helpful to give them a role in the church, where they can volunteer, but that keeps them from being too emotionally heavy with other people.

Understanding The Unchurched

The gulf between the church and the world is widening. Church leaders need methods and strategies to seek to understand those they are trying to reach outside their walls.

"It is hard to overstate how ghettoized our preaching is. It is common to make all kinds of statements that appear persuasive to us but are based upon all sorts of premises that the secular person does not hold... Show a continual willingness to address the questions that the unbelieving heart will ask. Speak respectfully and sympathetically to people who have difficulty with Christianity... Listen to everything said in the worship service with the ears of someone who has doubts or troubles with belief."

-Tim Keller

"When you invite a friend who doesn't attend church to come with you to church, everything changes. Suddenly, you listen to the music differently... You start to wonder whether the message would make any sense to an outsider, and shudder if it's filled with language that's so 'churchy' you have to be a life-long Christian to understand it... You begin to notice things like the cracks in the sidewalk... You'll also see whether you have an easy on-ramp for new people who want to explore Christianity deeper. Many churches don't. They just have programs that work for those who already attend."

-Carey Nieuwhof

"I have become all things to all people so that by all possible means I might save some. I do all this for the sake of the gospel, that I may share in its blessings."

-1 Corinthians 9:22-23

Importance:
-No one can approach effective pastoral ministry without understanding secular people and the larger context that we minister

within. Ours is an increasingly "post-Christian" culture. There may be some regions where many people still attend church *en masse*- but even here, they are still being shaped primarily by secular values and narratives. (These regions will see the natural inclination toward church attendance decreasing as time rolls on.) It is essential for pastors to become master exegetes of these postures and narratives. Ironically, when you work at connecting with secular people, you will connect more meaningfully with many church people as well!

If secular people are not drawn to your ministry, you are not ministering in the Spirit of Jesus. If religious legalists are never offended by your ministry, you are not ministering in the Spirit of Jesus. Read the gospels — this pattern is clear.

Practical Strategies That Help Pastors "Get" Secular People:

-Find ways of simply hanging out with secular people: invite neighbors over and really listen to them, play poker monthly with the fellas, go to every party to which you may get invited. Parties where people are drinking too much and swearing too much are the ones that matter. "Truth serum" can teach you quite a bit about people.

-Read articles about *why* people don't believe or *why* they are leaving the church. Read articles written by sociologists and not only by frustrated churched young adults. Don't confuse their negative experiences with the values of secular people. These are two different sets of issues.

-Additionally, read sociology articles on the patterns and attitudes of Americans in general and how they are changing and why.

-Become familiar with the websites that many "normal" people in your local community visit regularly. This will be different for every community. Oklahoma is not California's Bay Area.

-Even better, watch the most popular movies and serial TV dramas, and listen to top 40 music. Overtime, you will begin to intuit how most people think and feel and live.

-Notice what trends on Twitter and the *Huffington Post*. Your outreach is limited by what you consume. If you only read Christian books and listen to Christian music, you will only reach Christians.

-Read very widely — read stuff you are not typically interested in.

-American history and the specific history of your local community is invaluable. It will show you how and why people see themselves, and their world, in the way that they do.

-Research local demographic changes and notice the patterns of the lives of local people. Additionally, pay attention to architecture. The largest local buildings scream out what matters most to the community. The way neighborhoods are designed shapes the patterns, habits, and even values of a people group. Pay attention to these.

-Consider volunteering where you can rub shoulders with normal people. And let your board and staff know that you are doing this. This will help to shape the culture of your church.

How To Use What You Learn:

-Whenever you are prepping a sermon, or Sunday worship, or designing your website, keep secular people in mind as if you were doing this *for them* — touching their values, using their language, explaining in a way that they would understand. This one thing has the potential to revolutionize your ministry. Bible commentaries should be the last thing you read. They are written by Bible scholars to other scholars or to academic students of the Bible. They rarely consider the outsider.

-Every decision your church makes should consider: *1. Radical commitment to Jesus* AND 2. *Radical hospitality to the secular person.* You need to keep both in mind. Everything should have the aroma of Jesus and be interesting to outsiders. These always go together.

-Regularly consider: *What about this local culture naturally connects with the kingdom of God?* Use these insights to build bridges with people - use these insights to shape the "public" image of your church. *What is this local community missing? How is it specifically hurting?* These insights should shape your church's service in the neighborhoods. *What about this local culture runs contrary to the kingdom of God?* These insights should shape your prophetic challenge. Consider all three of these questions.

-Purposefully find ways to run contrary to the negative stereotypes that people have of churches.

-In general, spend twice as much time worrying about boring or unnecessarily offending secular people than worrying about offending long-time church people.

Personal Growth For Pastors

Church leaders cannot take parishioners farther than they have grown. This section offers tips and tactics to keep oneself spiritually and emotionally healthy and maturing.

"Self-care is never a selfish act — it is simply good stewardship of the only gift I have, the gift I was put on earth to offer others. Anytime we can listen to true self and give the care it requires, we do it not only for ourselves, but for the many others whose lives we touch."

-Parker Palmer

"When you find a writer who really is saying something to you, read everything that writer has written... Then go to people who influenced that writer... and your world builds together in an organic way that is really marvelous."

-Joseph Campbell

"Very early in the morning, while it was still dark, Jesus got up, left the house and went off to a solitary place, where he prayed. Simon and his companions went to look for him, and when they found him, they exclaimed: 'Everyone is looking for you!'"

-Mark 1:35-37

Personal Formation
-Ministry necessarily involves consistently giving out to others: serving them, leading them, encouraging them, inspiring them. If the pastor is not *intentional* about self-care and formation, they will inevitably crash. And when they do, they will take way too many people out with them.

-The practices listed below may or may not be obvious ones, but they are *essential* for practicing church leaders. In fact, one could make a case that the most important thing that a church leader does is to *attend to their own personal formation*. If they do, not only will they keep from falling apart personally, but more importantly, the entire ministry will bear more and more fruit. You cannot under estimate the importance of an integrated and healthy senior leader.

-The following practices are not listed in any intentional order. They are all to be practiced simultaneously.

Seeing A Therapist Or Spiritual Director

-Family of origin issues, personal hang-ups, and past abuses and struggles, will all come out when engaged in the throes of ministry. (If they don't, one's implosion down the road is nearly guaranteed.) The wise church leader will choose to proactively see one of these professionals on a monthly basis. It may be the only context where the pastor can be completely honest and dump everything on to another person. Exploring why one does, what they do peculiarly, can save one from hurting themselves and others in the long run.

-Additionally, when many church leaders begin this practice, they are amazed at how much it adds to their understanding of the Bible. The modern world is a disintegrated place. When one begins to address the hidden parts of the person, the sacred text seems to pop in 3D.

Working Out (And Sleeping When You Can)

-Pastors rarely use their bodies but the Son of God showed up in one. Church leaders who do not attend to their bodies (particularly with weight-lifting) often feel personally weak and fearful. Church leaders who work out find that their visions grow, their confidence in what's possible grows, and their willingness to take on difficult issues grows. (It's also a natural anti-depressant.) Finally, leaders gain more respect from other people when they take care of themselves.

-Sleep really, really matters. It is hard to love people when you are tired. But ministry doesn't always allow for it. Soldier on when necessary, but then when things calm down, get caught up on sleep. It typically takes three or four days of solid sleep to make up for a day with very little. The older you get, the more important this will be. Often people realize, by their mid-thirties, that their ability to "keep going" without sleep diminishes significantly.

Talking With Close Friends OUTSIDE Of The Ministry

-Everyone needs friends and church leaders should certainly be friendly with the people who are members of their church. But professionally and ethically, there is much that a pastor cannot share with them. (Private matters, your personal feelings about the church, and so forth.) Therefore, it is essential to have close friends *outside* of the ministry. This does not accidentally happen. It must be purposefully pursued. Church work has a way of dominating one's social life. Many times, church leaders who have affairs are isolated individuals who have few friends that they can process things with. Besides, when you move on from the church, or when you retire, you will find yourself utterly alone if you have not cultivated other friendships. You believe that the people in your church love you as a person — but the reality is, they love the role that you play among them. When the role ends, many times the relationships end.

Scripture Meditation, Prayer, And Retreats
-It is too easy to be in scripture only when prepping a sermon. The long-haul pastor needs personal time with God — just for them. There is not one right way to do this. Figure out a form that works for you. It is likely, that this "form" will change multiple times over your ministry. But make it a priority.

-Additionally, one day a month at a retreat center, or at a local park to personally be alone with God does wonders. Plan it ahead in your schedule.

-*A final note:* everything listed above will seem impossible if you don't personally own your schedule. There won't be time. *You must plan these activities into your schedule before you plan out the church calendar.* If you do, you will be surprised at how much you can get done — thanks to being personally full and healthy. If you don't, you will feel like you are short on time and you will feel weak and overwhelmed. *Your primary ministry is to be the healthiest person in your church. NOT to be doing the most!*

Lifelong Learning

Self-Directed Reading And Learning:
-The adage is a true one: *the leader is a reader*. Continual learning and reading offers many benefits:

1. The more you learn, the more angles you will have at your disposal to frame problems and possible solutions.

2. A church will not grow beyond the pastor. For a church to keep growing (numerically, spiritually, relationally, and in other ways) the pastor must keep growing.

3. It is nearly impossible to reach anyone who, in general, is more well-read than you are. Pastors must stay ahead to be able to offer real solutions to inquisitive types and to be able to connect with all kinds of people.

-The wise pastor will read much more than ministry books. They will purposefully read about cultural developments, sociology, psychology, theology, non-profit leadership and management, novels, and popular stuff that are all the rage of the moment. If you cannot always read books, articles, and book reviews will work nearly as well. *The New York Times Book Review*, *the New York Review of Books*, and *the Times Literary Supplement* can give you a quick review of all the new ideas and vibes coming down the pike. *Christianity Today* and *Christian Century* will keep you abreast of current ministry trends. Pay attention to best sellers, popular movies, and music and serial television programs as well.

-Thoughtful podcasts and YouTube videos are also convenient and helpful.

Learning From Others:
-Ministry seminars have some utility; however, they can also push faddish trends and lead some ministers to feel like failures compared to the megachurch presenters or the hipster innovators. In general, if you tend to be idealistic and bookish, you need to attend some ministry seminars to see what is working and to keep from being too "out of it". The trends that will be promoted are working for a reason. Learn from them. However, if you are a mainstream evangelical in a megachurch, you might want to avoid them and read more to become a little deeper. Work against your default posture to keep growing and learning.

-Seeking out a more experienced pastor who leads a church larger than yours is a wise move. You will glean honest reflections that will keep you moving forward.

-Additionally, seek out an older business leader as a mentor. A church is not the same thing as a business. But many seminary trained pastors struggle with organizational realities and these mentors can provide practical guidance. They will help you to learn to lead in such a way that professional people with good jobs and money will get excited about backing you and your ministry. This is crucial.

-If you find it stimulating to follow some "big name" pastors from afar, try to follow ones that seem to have a similar personality to yours and who pastor in a similar location to yours. Trying to emulate someone who is completely different from you, in an altogether different context, is fools' gold.

-In general, it is a good idea to have many different mentors (local and afar). This will help you to find your own voice.

-A couple of times a year (on vacation or whenever) visit a church that is radically different from your own. You will catch some helpful ideas that may stimulate your thinking.

-Consider having the church hire a personal coach to meet with you or talk with you on the phone, or through video conferening once a month. You will learn quite a bit, you will be able to process things aloud that you cannot with your own board or staff, and it will communicate to your board that you are serious about continually developing your skills and knowledge base. At times, it may be helpful to have them visit a board meeting or two at your church, or meet with your staff, to offer some even more specific feedback. They will notice things that you are too "close" to see. They can say things that you cannot say. They will also then be able to coach you with more effectiveness as they gain more of an insider's view of your ministry.

Skill Development:
-Pastors who can effectively lead for decades give serious attention to skill development: preaching, leading meetings, counseling, overseeing and training staff, etc. To keep growing with a ministry — skill development will be a lifelong journey.

-The basic pattern of skill development is rather simple and yet alarming effective:
1. Simply act (preach a sermon, lead a meeting, and so on).
2. Evaluate — give serious attention to what worked, what didn't work, why, and the like.
3. Readjust your approach.
4. Try again.
5. Keep repeating.

Self-Awareness And Time Management

No two pastors are the same. Understanding who one is, and how to effectively manage one's strengths and weakness is essential.

"Without knowledge of self, there is no knowledge of God."

-John Calvin

"Knowing ourselves is something so important that I wouldn't want any relaxation ever in this regard, however high you may have climbed to the heavens... So I repeat that it is good, indeed very good, to try to enter first into the room where self-knowledge is dealt with rather than to fly off to other rooms... In my opinion we shall never completely know ourselves if we don't strive to know God."

-Teresa of Avila

"Do not think of yourself more highly than you ought, but rather think of yourself with sober judgment, in accordance with the faith God has distributed to each of you. For just as each of us has one body with many members, and these members do not all have the same function, so in Christ we, though many, form one body, and each member belongs to all the others. We have different gifts, according to the grace given to each of us."

-Romans 12:3-6

The Importance Of Self-Awareness:
-The myth of the pastor who can "do it all" is dangerous for the pastor as an individual and often has a negative impact on the ministry. Nearly every pastor excels at a couple of things, is "okay" at other things, and is woefully deficient in other things.
-If you are aware of your strengths and weaknesses, you can operate most helpfully for the ministry *and* model humble and appropriate self-understanding for others.

How To Grow In Self-Awareness:
-First of all (and possibly most importantly) acknowledge to yourself

that you have a *particular* way of being and recognize that you are *not* just like everyone else. Recognizing this is half of the battle. You have a *particular* approach and angle that is unique and needed yet is also not the most accurate perspective. Seek out to understand yourself as *others* see you.

-Be curious and take note of what sorts of things that people compliment you for, what types of things people accuse you of, and what sorts of things never generate compliments or condemnations. What people compliment you on *and* what they chide you for likely reveal your God-given abilities. (A gift can be used to help or harm others. Used wisely it is a blessing. In its raw form its often off-putting.) What people never say much about at all is likely a non-gift.

-Take various personality tests (Myers-Briggs, Enneagram, The Big Five, Strengths-Finder, and others) and look for common themes. Get personal feedback from others concerning your test results.

-Seek out personal therapy and/or personal mentoring from and experienced leader and listen to what they tell you — *about you.*

How To Use Your Learned Self-Awareness:

-Whatever you are gifted at should be how you invest 50 – 70% of your time as a pastor. This will bring real value to the ministry. It could be caring for and relating to individuals, organizing activities, providing real leadership, preaching and teaching, offering counseling, or other talents. Whatever it is, make it the main thrust of your personal ministry. (Don't imitate what others are doing.) But to be sure, you will need to develop this gift: take classes on the subject, read books, secure a mentor who is also known for these particular skills, and more.

-Recognize that *much more* than your personal gift(s) are needed for the ministry to thrive! Hire people and recruit key volunteers who have very *different* gifts than you have. Celebrate them and value them. Be honest about your strengths and weaknesses and how the ministry needs *different people.* This will greatly enhance the overall ministry and create real harmony between various individuals within the church.

-Give serious attention to making sure that the extremes of your personality do not harm the ministry. If you are an intellectual, make sure that your preaching does not devolve into lecturing. If you are a people-person, make sure that you do an appropriate amount of managing and leading and not simply connecting. If you are a leader, make sure that you are careful to treat people with care and not run over them on the way to implementing your vision.

-You are, who you are, for a reason. God created you with a specific role to play. However, you must learn to steward your gifts with wisdom. Your talents are probably helpful guides as to how you ought to operate as a church leader, but beware, they are not salvific. What you personally need, spiritually and psychologically as an individual, is likely not more and more freedom to wallow in your own personality. The Spirit is concerned more with your integration that that.

Planning:

-You will likely need an hour each week to simply plan out your next week in detail and sketch out how you will use the next week or two after that. (This is best accomplished on the weekend and not waiting until Monday morning.) Once you have served in ministry for some time, you will have an idea of how long sermon preparation takes, preparing for meetings, and all that goes with that. Make it a priority to get these regular tasks on your calendar ahead of time. If you don't, unimportant but "urgent" tasks will fill up your calendar.

-Split your days into thirds: mornings, afternoons, and evenings. (This leaves you with 21 "time periods" for the week.) In general, the church should get eleven of your "time periods." Thus, if you have meetings and work in the evening, feel free to either spend the morning or the afternoon at home. If for two days in a row you had to work morning, afternoon, and evening, take the third day off — even if it's not scheduled. Some weeks will require more, some less, but work to have this as your typical goal.

-Most tasks can be completed in about half of the amount of time that you might assume, if you think them through and plan efficiently. It is worth taking the time to plan the most efficient way to do something. For example, do all the hospital visitations and/or visiting of shut-ins on the same trip away from the office and base your personal moments of scripture mediation and prayer on the same passage that you will preaching that Sunday, and other similar things.

-In general, your first priority is personal time with God. Next, give attention to whichever is *harder* for you to do: working on projects or people work. Lastly, do whatever is naturally *easiest* for you: working on projects or people work.

-The "typical" pastor likely spends one day a week in staff meetings plus meeting one on one with staff members. One day is likely spent in pastoral care: hospital visitations, counseling, wedding prep, and so on. One day is spent in working on leadership projects and initiatives, preparing for board meetings, and more, and around two days prepping their sermon and preparing for Sunday worship.

-Learn to see your time in "weeks rather than days." Nearly every day will be imbalanced — but work should generally balance out over a week. Some days you will be so busy, you will not have time to personally spend time in prayer. Some days you won't see your family at all. But over a whole week — there should be balance.

Principles Of Time Management In Ministry:

-You serve the church and your family, by working hard to only do the things that must be done by you. (That list is much smaller than many pastors realize.)

-Things that *only* the pastor can do: cast and keep the vision, lead the church board, lead the staff, emphasize outreach and social justice, see to it that are leaders are being developed, exemplify the values, and serve as the main representative of the church to the surrounding community. (Most other things can be delegated.)

-You need to intentionally "teach" people to respect your time. Do not drop everything every time someone wants to see you. This trains people to expect that you are always available. Unless it is a true emergency, calls should be returned the next day and plans can be made to get together within a week or so.

-Pastors who cannot say "no" or slightly disappoint others, often believe they are living as servants. They are not. They are slaves to the urgent over the important. They will be praised in the moment but it will hurt the ministry over time. They will suffer the pain of knowing that much of their energy and talents have been wasted on other people's plans and on trivial matters.

-One of the blessings of ministry is that you have a fair amount of flexibility in how you use your time, when you work, etc. However, this can also be a curse. Tread carefully. It is certainly possible to spend too much time on ministry and to neglect your family. It is also possible to spend too much time with your family and to neglect the ministry. All things being equal, the church should receive a full week from you (45-50 hours) and a few extra hours for worship and church gatherings. (If you assume that lay people should work full-time and give time to the church, so should you.)

Interviewing For A Position And Befriending A Denomination

Here, the reader dives into the tactics of applying for a position. Additionally, advice is given in relating effectively to larger ecclesiastical bodies.

"Perhaps some of us have to go through dark and devious ways before we can find the river of peace or the highroad to the soul's destination."

-Joseph Campbell

Vocation is "living a life congruent with who we are, how God has gifted us, graced us and thus called us... That said, it is in our communal associations with others that we find ourselves... Self-knowledge happens best in community."

-Gordon T. Smith

"When they came to the border of Mysia, they tried to enter Bithyia, but the Spirit of Jesus would not allow them to. So they passed by Mysia and went down to Troas. During the night Paul had a vision of a man of Macedonia standing and begging him, 'Come over to Macedonia and help us.'"

-Acts 16:7-9

Applying For A Position
-Tailor your resume for *each specific church position* that you apply for. Generic resumes carry very little punch. Study the church's website in depth, listen to their sermon podcasts, be sure to use "their language" in the resume.

-To create a solid resume, you will need to work at doing what you typically should *not* do: brainstorm everything that you have accomplished or experienced and find a way to list them positively! Things such as serving as a junior high youth group volunteer should be described as: *"Served as Key Leader of Teen Ministry — providing leadership in everything from counseling teens, planning and preparing for youth worship experiences, organizing outreaches to unbelieving teens- all the while being personally mentored by the senior pastor and meeting with them one-on-one every week. "* See the difference? You cannot and should not *lie* — but you should describe everything in rather positive terms. In sending a resume, the goal is to be invited further into the process. Crafting a thorough resume, tailored for the recipient, goes a long way in getting invited further along.

-Be sure to include a cover letter (today it's often the body of the email with your resume attached.) Cover letters are often a *bit* more personal and should reveal a little bit of your personality. They be a little more informal. But always be polite and professional. The goal of the cover letter is to help you to appear likable, and a good enough fit, that someone should read through resume. Everything needs to be completed with an eye towards being mistake-free. Resume mistakes connote a lack of professionalism to potential employers.

-Send out several resumes (all individually tailored for each church). An experienced minister, with proven gifts, may move to the "next" stage (after sending in their resume) in maybe half of the churches they apply to. They may also be asked to personally interview in half of those situations. They may be formally offered a position in half of the churches in which they interview. So even a veteran minister may have to apply to 8 churches to receive a formal job offer. How many churches may you need to apply to? A well-advertised senior pastor position may expect 150-250 applications. The average youth pastor position often receives well over 100 applications. This is a numbers game. *You cannot apply to too many positions.* What is the worst that can happen? More than one church is interested in you and you must pick which one where you would like to serve? Typically, new ministry job seekers do not cast the net wide enough when looking for a position.

-Popular websites liist pastoral vacancies. Larger seminaries may offer job boards listing multiple positions from all over the country. Vanderbloemen.com, Slingshotgroup.org, and Ministersearch.com are professional, ministry-based, search firms. Additionally, most denominations (if you are willing to dig through their websites) list open positions. Look through any denomination, that in any way, is related to the current one in which you are serving. Many openings can be found through Google Jobs.

-With this said, most people still find positions through people that they know. As much as you want to tailor a resume for every church in which you apply, it may still be helpful to create a general resume and send it out to any pastors, ministry leaders, denominational leaders, or contacts you have in the field and ask them to pass it on to anyone they know who is looking to hire someone.

-Remember: it is much easier to find a position if you are willing to relocate. Deciding that you only want to minister within a particular city, or region, will severely limit your options. In general, the quickest way to "advance" in any career is through a willingness to relocate.

The Next Steps

-If the church likes your resume, many times, you will be asked to answer some essay questions, in which the church board will ask you your opinion or philosophy of ministry on various topics.

-Sample questions may include: *Why are you applying to serve at our church? Describe a time when you led someone to a personal relationship with Jesus Christ? Describe your views of Biblical Creation vs. Evolution. What is your opinion of women in ministry?* and more.

-You cannot or should not lie in answering these questions. This is not helpful for you or the church (and of course it is unethical). However, choose your words *carefully*. From studying their website, you should have a good handle on where the church is coming from on these issues and the particular vocabulary that the church uses. Sometimes, you may find that you and the church do not have radically different positions, but you use different vocabularies. (For example, some churches say that they are egalitarian, they maintain that men and women are equal in the eyes of God and are free to serve as leaders in the church. In other contexts, some churches mean the same thing, but instead of using the word "egalitarian", they use the word "feminist". In different contexts, one word seems to fit- where another is not used. If you study the church's website and documents, you should be able to tell if you would truly not fit them and where you may simply need to adjust to their vocabulary.)

-Remember, the goal in answering these questions is not to baldly share what you believe about every issue or doctrine. *Your goal is to show that you are similar enough to the church that you may be asked to interview*. This requires a wise form of dancing. You do not want to misrepresent yourself. But you also do not want to share "everything" that you believe. There is not a gainfully employed pastor that shares "everything" that they believe with their congregation! This is not what a pastor does. However, you do want to be sure that you are not dramatically opposed to where the church is coming from.

Interviewing

-Typically, today, the first interview is via video conferencing. Dress as if you were meeting them in person. Be friendly — *the main point of this interview is for them to decide if they like you* (and if you like them). Be humble, yet confident. Carry yourself as if you *were already* their pastor. (Not just being yourself — but being *pastoral*.) Be sure that you look at the camera on your laptop and not the screen. If you look at the camera it appears like you are looking at them in the eye. If you look at the screen, you appear to always be looking down! You should be able to generally share your philosophy of ministry but beware of offering some "grand vision" for them. (Though they will often ask you for it.) The best answer tends to be: *"All ministry is local. I would have to be there with you for a year, getting to know you and the local community, before any kind of future vision would emerge."* Be sure to ask the search committee plenty of questions. You are interviewing them too.

-The second interview tends to get down to business a little more. It's a little more honest and direct.

-If you *are* offered a job, it is customary for them to give you a week or two to decide if you would like to accept it. If any negotiation needs to be made (salary, start date, and the like) wait to do this until *after* you have officially been offered a job and contract. (It is generally not a good idea to inquire about the salary until you are offered a position.) It is fine for you to ask for the phone number of the former pastor or staff member, that you will be potentially replacing, during this time. Be sure to call your predecessor and ask them about their opinions of the church.

-Just because you are offered a position doesn't mean you need to accept it. It is not unethical to turn it down if offered. The goal of the whole application/interview process is for you to be offered the job and then you can decide accordingly.

A Few Odds And Ends

-It's often a poor idea to share with a present employer that you are interviewing somewhere else. *Only inform them if you accept a job offer.* But be prepared — some churches will dismiss you immediately.

Others, may expect a four-month notice. (Especially for senior pastor roles.) Every church handles this differently. Additionally, some consider it unethical to purposefully leave a position at one church, to take a position at another church, within the same town. (Your "followers" will likely follow you to that church.) The only exception may be a clear move "up" (such as leaving one church as youth pastor to take a senior pastor role at another one).

-In general, after sending in a resume, its bad form to inquire of your status. If they are interested, they will contact you. Many won't. Some may even take several weeks to get back to you even if they are interested. (Church search committees tend to move rather slowly.) However, if you make it to the next level (such as filling out a questionnaire) it's fine to send a quick email after about three weeks or so and inquire about the status of the position if you have not heard from them all. This may show them that you are very interested in the position.

-A few things to never do: ask what the position pays (you will find out when they offer you the job), insult the church or imply that they "don't get it," assume that the church is dying to have you, or conversely, to appear desperate for a job.

Value Of A Denomination

-Independent churches are legitimate and can be a very valid biblical expression of the body of Christ. However, they can also miss out on much that a denomination can offer.

-It is a good posture (most especially for a younger pastor) to submit to a *larger tradition*. It is helpful to have a group much larger than your specific church who endorses you, supports you, guides you, and teaches you. The temptation for narcissistic driven ministry is strong in young pastors. Denominations can push against this. Additionally, being part of a larger network of churches quickly communicates to outsiders that your church is not a cult.

-Denominations can easily give you access to experienced mentors and coaches that you can learn from. And possibly one day, that will also provide a platform for you to build into the next generation after you.

-Denominational involvement can generate real appreciation for the diversity of the body of Christ. You will meet pastors and church leaders who do ministry very differently than you do, and yet, God still uses them. This will also help you to discern your larger place in the body of

186

Christ — by noticing how you compare with everyone else (in a healthy way).

-If you are involved with a denomination, your church may also receive favorable loans and grants that you could not receive at a bank. Many times, you might find cheaper health insurance, retirement plans, and more.

-Finally, if you are plugged in denominationally — you have a natural network. If you decide it is time to move on and find another post, it is much easier within a denomination. It is also much easier for your church to find your replacement after you leave.

How To Interact With Your Denomination

-When pursuing licensure and/or ordination, this is not a time for you to share with complete transparency, every little thing you believe, or don't believe, and why. These exams or written statements are meant for you to prove that you *fit* the denomination. There is a difference between sharing every thought that you have and learning to play well with others. Remember this.

-In general, you should attend all events that are designed for pastors. This is part of being a team player and building pastoral collegiality.

-When engaging with others, be friendly, respectful, work to get along well with everyone. These are not gatherings for you to push your specific agendas or to strongly voice your opinions — these are times for bridge-building.

-When corporate decisions are being made by you and other pastors, try your best to not push your personal preferences. Attempt to think and pray through what may be best for the entire denomination.

-On the other hand, do not feel like you need to push denominational events to your entire church unless they would be helpful for your specific congregation. Not all corporate events are helpful for every specific church.

-It is typically a good idea to serve in one role for the denomination. You stand on the shoulders of others who served before you came along. You wouldn't be here without them. It is honorable for you to also do your part. However, just one role. Some can easily become sidetracked from their specific church ministry as they volunteer within the denomination. Particularly if their church is plateaued or struggling, the denomination can become a welcomed distraction. This is understandable, but rarely helpful.

About The Author

Brian A. Ross is Assistant Professor of Pastoral Ministries at the Fresno Pacific Biblical Seminary and the editor of *Signs of the Times: Pastoral Translations of Ministry And Culture in Honor of Leonard I. Sweet*. He has over twenty years of ministry experience, having served as a youth pastor, church planter, senior pastor, teaching pastor, and church consultant. He is a minister with the Brethren in Christ Church and currently serves as a volunteer leader in a new church plant.